MATH MYSTERIES

MATH MYSTERIES

Stories and Activities to Build Problem-Solving Skills
by Jack Silbert

SCHOLASTIC
PROFESSIONAL BOOKS

New York ◆ Toronto ◆ London ◆ Auckland ◆ Sydney

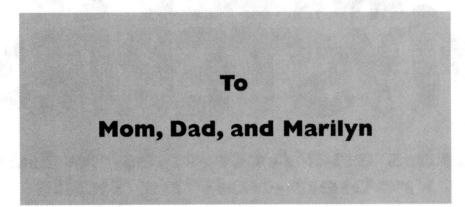

To

Mom, Dad, and Marilyn

Cover design by Vincent Ceci and Jaime Lucero
Cover and interior illustrations by Hank Morehouse
Interior design by Ellen Matlach Hassell,
Boultinghouse & Boultinghouse

ISBN # 0-590-60337-X
Copyright © 1995 by Jack Silbert
All rights reserved.
Printed in the U.S.A.

12 11 10 9 8   8 9/9

Table of Contents

◆ Introduction ◆

Welcome to Math Mysteries! In the following pages, your students will meet the staff of the Effective Detective Agency: Cesar Hidalgo, Carmen Chang, Gina Jasper, Chuck McBuck, and Tommy Tompkins. These young detectives face some of the zaniest cases you'll ever see. All the while, they'll be teaching your students valuable problem solving skills and strategies.

The Stories

A humorous reproducible story begins each lesson. The detectives need to use problem-solving skills and strategies to crack each wacky case. In their laugh-filled adventures, they'll walk your students through each problem-solving method, step by step. The stories will motivate your students to complete the exercises that follow.

The Questions

Each story is followed by a series of engaging math questions. Students use the problem-solving techniques they have just learned to help the detectives, to solve additional cases, and to make sense of other kooky situations.

In addition to problem-solving practice, there are also open-ended questions that promote critical thinking, writing in math, cooperative learning activities, and more.

Teaching Notes

Before each story is a section entitled "For the Teacher." This section points out the featured problem-solving skill or strategy in the following story. There is a comprehensive list of additional computation and problem-solving skills covered in the lesson. There is a story summary and a brief explanation of what students will be asked to do. Last but not least, this section discusses the problem-solving skill, mentions real-life applications, provides hints for the students, suggests discussion topics, and more.

FOR THE TEACHER

A Soup-er Code

Story Summary
Detective Tommy Tompkins cracks a phone code to get back the costume of Soup Man, the local superhero.

The Questions
Students use the phone code to decode rhyming messages from the thief.

Teaching Notes
Students may think this is a fun puzzle and be very surprised to find out that there is math involved. Actually, this activity exposes students to several problem-solving strategies. When they write down the possible letters for each number, they are "making a list." When they try to pick which letters are correct, they are "guessing and checking" and "using logic." It is an engaging way to use numbers and motivate students to think.

SKILL/STRATEGY

Solving a code

Additional Skills:
- Making a list
- Using logic
- Guess and check

2	6	9	5
A	M	W	J
B	N	X	K
C	O	Y	L

I want to meet you in person;
That really is my secret goal.
You like football and love soup.
Let's meet before the Soup-er 2695.

A Soup-er Code — 11

FOR THE TEACHER

The Cafeteria Caper

Story Summary
Detective Carmen Chang takes a sample of students in a school to estimate the number of suspects in a cafeteria case.

The Questions
Students use their class as a sample and predict the number of students in the entire school who have a variety of characteristics.

SKILL/STRATEGY

Taking a sample

Additional Skills:
- Gathering data
- Whole number ×
- Estimation
- Finding attributes

Teaching Notes
Taking a sample is an extremely useful statistical tool. The process can yield accurate predictions while saving a tremendous amount of time. Explain to students that whenever they see survey results, only a small portion of the population was actually questioned. The more people that are surveyed, the more accurate the results.

This lesson can also serve as a basic introduction to ratios and proportions. Let's say there are 5 redheads in a class of 30. The ratio of redheads to students in the class is 5:30, or $5/30$, or $1/6$. If there are 300 students in the school, a proportion can be written to estimate the number of redheads in the school:

$$\frac{1 \text{ redhead}}{6 \text{ students}} = \frac{x \text{ redheads}}{300 \text{ students}}$$

By cross multiplying, we can estimate that there are 50 redheads in the entire school.

The Cafeteria Caper — 79

The Organization

In general, easier skills come earlier in the book, and more difficult ones come later. However, you may wish to pick and choose from the entire book, depending on your particular curriculum.

Additional Materials

This book is designed to "stand alone": Your students will not need any additional materials to complete the exercises (besides a pencil and additional paper).

Many of the lessons are suitable for calculator use.

Problem Solving

Problem solving is one of the most important areas of mathematics today. The National Council of Teachers of Mathematics has named problem solving as Standard Number One on its list of curriculum standards. The goal is for students to develop and apply a variety of strategies to solve problems—routine and nonroutine. They will see mathematics in the world around them and know how to approach it. They will know there is more than one way to solve a problem (and often, more than one solution!).

The strategies presented in this book will inspire students to look at problems from many perspectives and to work through them in a logical manner.

Computation

While problem solving has become a "buzzword" in the mathematics world, no one has forgotten the importance of traditional computation. The stories and lessons in this book cover a wide variety of computation skills. The "For the Teacher" Additional Skills section before each story lists the skills covered within.

Computation Key

+ = addition

− = subtraction

× = multiplication

÷ = division

Other concepts covered in the book include working with time, working with money, measurement, geometry, working with decimals, introduction to fractions, and much more.

The Answers

A complete answer key is located at the back of the book.

I hope this book helps you to motivate your students in developing the crucial problem-solving strategies they need. And I hope they have a great time doing it!

Jack Silbert

A Soup-er Code

Story Summary

Detective Tommy Tompkins cracks a phone code to get back the costume of Soup Man, the local superhero.

The Questions

Students use the phone code to decode rhyming messages from the thief.

Teaching Notes

Students may think this is a fun puzzle and be very surprised to find out that there is math involved. Actually, this activity exposes students to several problem-solving strategies. When they write down the possible letters for each number, they are "making a list." When they try to pick which letters are correct, they are "guessing and checking" and "using logic." It is an engaging way to use numbers and motivate students to think.

```
2   6   9   5
A   M   W   J
B   N   X   K
C   O   Y   L
```

I want to meet you in person;
That really is my secret goal.
You like football and love soup.
Let's meet before the Soup-er 2695.

◆ A Soup-er Code ◆

My name is Tommy Tompkins. My friends and I started the Effective Detective Agency. Cesar, Gina, Chuck, Carmen, and I are some of the best detectives around (even if we're only kids!). We have to be good, too, because we get some crazy cases.

Take the other day, for example. I was sitting at my desk, getting ready to bite into a big sandwich: the Tommy Salami Special. Just then, a man wearing a gray suit and glasses came into the Effective Detective Agency office.

"Can you help me?" he asked.

I looked around. I was too busy to help this man. My sandwich was all ready! But it looked like I was the only detective in the office. "I guess so," I said, placing the Tommy Salami Special in my desk drawer. "What's your name?"

"You probably have heard of me," said the man. "I am...Soup Man!"

"You are not Soup Man," I said. Soup Man was our local superhero. "Soup Man is a tall, strong guy, with a red cape. And a big soup can costume."

"That's why I'm here," said the man. "My real name is Cluck Kant. I normally change into my Soup Man costume in a phone booth. The one on the corner of Elm Street and Main. When I went by there today, the phone booth was gone."

"There are phone booths all over town. Find another place to change into your suit," I said. Another day's work was done, and I could get back to my sandwich.

"You don't understand," Cluck cried. "My costume was in that booth. Without the giant soup can, I have no Super Soup powers! Whoever stole that phone booth is trying to ruin me."

This looked like a serious problem. The Tommy Salami would have to wait. "Were there any clues at the scene of the crime?" I asked.

Cluck pulled a piece of paper out of his pocket. "I found this note that tells me how to get my costume back. But I can't understand it," he said.

I took the note from Cluck. Sure enough, some of the words had been replaced with numbers. It was a secret code. The beginning of the note told what day Cluck could meet the thief:

I want to meet you in person;
That really is my secret goal.
You like football and love soup.
Let's meet before the Soup-er 2695.

I stared at the numbers, and tried to figure out the code. Suddenly, it hit me. "I've got it!" I said. "Someone who stole a phone booth would probably use a phone code." Each number in the code stood for a letter on the

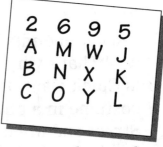

phone buttons. Underneath each number, I wrote down the three letters each number could stand for:

Now all I had to do was circle one letter under each number. The answer should spell out a word that makes sense in the note.

Cluck shook my hand. "I'm glad you cracked the code. I really thought I was in hot water," he said. "But soon I'll be back in hot soup."

NOW IT'S YOUR TURN...

Help Tommy solve the case. Use the phone buttons at right to help you. In questions 1 through 4, use Tommy's phone code to figure out the secret messages in the thief's note. First write down the possible letters under each number in the message. Then circle one letter under each number to spell out a word. Write that word in the "Answer" blank.

1. I want to meet you in person;
That really is my secret goal.
You like football and love soup.
Let's meet before the Soup-er   2   6   9   5.

Possible letters: ___ ___ ___ ___

___ ___ ___ ___

___ ___ ___ ___

Answer: ___ ___ ___ ___

2. I'm sorry about your phone booth;
   Now you can't make a call.
   But you'll get your phone booth back,
   If you meet me outside City   4   2   5   5.

   Possible letters: __ __ __ __

                                     __ __ __ __

                                     __ __ __ __

   Answer: __ __ __ __

3. I'll give back your red cape,
   your soup can, and your sock.
   Just be sure that you're not late;
   I'll be there at   6   6   3   o'clock.

   Possible letters: __ __ __

                              __ __ __

                              __ __ __

   Answer: __ __ __

4. How will you know who I am?
   I think you'll recognize me soon.
   Then you'll know that I'm a friend—
   I'll be dressed as a giant 7   7   6   6   6.

   Possible letters: __ __ __ __ __

                                  __ __ __ __ __

                                  __ __ __ __ __

   Answer: __ __ __ __ __

	ABC	DEF
1	**2**	**3**
GHI	JKL	MNO
4	**5**	**6**
PRS	TUV	WXY
7	**8**	**9**
*	Oper **0**	**#**

5. In this phone code, which numbers on the phone cannot be used? _____

6. Which letters cannot be used in the phone code? _____

_____

YOU CAN DO IT Make up your own secret messages using the phone code. Trade them with friends and have them try to figure out the messages!

A Small Misunderstanding

Story Summary

Detective Gina Jasper tries to make sure that her detective trainee understands the problems while investigating a pencil robbery.

The Questions

Students read word problems, decide what is being asked, and finally solve the problems.

Teaching Notes

There are many ways to solve most math problems. This book presents several of those approaches. However, all of these methods are useless if a student does not understand the problem. This is not uncommon in word and story problems, where the actual math question is often hidden in a lot of text. In life, as well, the math problems are not always standing out in bold type. Sometimes it takes a little thinking to decide what information is really wanted.

Students will often come up with a flawless, original solution to a problem. Sadly, sometimes they are not answering the question that was asked! Stress the importance of reading problems slowly and carefully.

SKILL/STRATEGY

Understanding the problem

Additional Skills:
◆ Reading for detail
◆ Whole number +, −, ×, ÷
◆ Money/decimal ×
◆ Multistep problems
◆ Critical thinking

◆ A Small Misunderstanding ◆

We're all good friends here at the Effective Detective Agency. Between me, Tommy, Chuck, Carmen, and Cesar, there's no mystery we can't figure out. A lot of kids want to join our agency, but we always turn **them** away. That is, until Alfred showed up. Every day for three weeks, Alfred hung out in front of our offices. He said that being a detective was his only dream. "Please, please, please, Gina, let me be a detective!" he would whine. Finally, I gave in.

"Okay, Alfred, I'll teach you to be a detective," I said. "But only if you stop being so annoying."

"I promise," said Alfred. "Do I get my magnifying glass now? Do I? Do I?"

Telling Alfred to stop being annoying was like telling the sky to stop being blue! But I decided to give him one chance. I took Alfred along to Penny's Pencil Pit, a local pencil store. Penny told me that someone was stealing pencils. I thought I'd show Alfred how to investigate a case.

"What are we doing here?" asked Alfred. "Are we going to buy pencils? Do detectives need pencils? Why don't you use pens?"

"We're here because there was a robbery!" I said. Alfred was one confused kid. I tried to stay calm.

Penny was behind the counter when we entered the store. She told us that pencils had been stolen on Monday, Tuesday, and Wednesday.

"Did anyone else work in the store on those days, Penny?" I asked.

"No," said Penny, "just me."

"Ah-ha!" yelled Alfred. "She's the thief! Penny just admitted that she was in the store on Monday, Tuesday, and Wednesday! And pencils were stolen on those three days! If she was the only one here, then she must have taken the pencils! Let's take her to the police station, Gina! Wow, being a detective is easy."

"Penny, just ignore this little guy," I said, trying to smile. "Would you excuse us for a minute?"

I pulled Alfred by the ear to the back of the store. "I don't think Penny stole the pencils! Penny is an old friend of ours. Let me do the detective work. Just try to keep quiet, and maybe you'll learn something." Stay calm, Gina, I told myself.

"So why did you ask if anyone else worked here?" asked Alfred.

"I wanted to find out if we needed to question anyone else!" I said. "Alfred, when you're a detective, it's very important to understand the question."

"I'm sorry, Gina," said Alfred.

"It's okay," I said. "Now let's try this again."

We went back to the counter. "Penny, do you know how many pencils were stolen?" I asked.

"Yes. I count the pencils every day," she said. "On Monday, 11 pencils were stolen. On Tuesday, 6 pencils were stolen. And on Wednesday, 10 pencils were stolen."

"Okay, Alfred, now is your chance to help," I said to my detective-in-training. "I need to know how many pencils were stolen in all. How could we figure it out?"

"That's easy," said Alfred. "If 11 pencils were stolen on Monday, and 10 pencils were stolen on Wednesday, then we just subtract 10 from 11."

"That's wrong, Alfred," I said. "Try again."

"Now I remember how to do it," said Alfred. "Just multiply 10 times 6. And then divide by 11."

"Wrong again, Alfred," I said.

Alfred frowned. "I could figure this out if you'd give me my magnifying glass."

"Alfred, remember what I told you," I said. "If you want to be a detective, you have to understand the question. Penny told us that 11 pencils were stolen on Monday, 6 pencils on Tuesday, and 10 pencils on Wednesday. To find the total number of pencils, we add up the number of pencils. We know that 11 plus 6 plus 10 equals 27. So 27 pencils were stolen. Understand, Alfred? Okay, are you ready for the next question?"

"I'm going home," Alfred said. "I don't want to be a detective anymore. I want to be a fireman."

Alfred walked out the door. At least he finally understood: A good detective, just like a good pencil, has to be sharp.

NOW IT'S YOUR TURN...

Don't answer the following questions just yet. First, read them over carefully. Make sure you understand them. Then circle the letter next to the phrase that best explains how to answer the question. (Gina hopes your pencil isn't missing!)

1. Penny had 100 pencils in her display case at the beginning of the week. By Wednesday, 27 pencils had been stolen. How many pencils were still in the case?

◆ What could you do to answer the question?
   a. Add 100 and 27.
   b. Multiply 27 times 3.
   c. Subtract 27 from 100.

2. Penny charges $.05 each for her pencils. How much money could she have made from the 27 stolen pencils?

◆ What could you do to answer the question?
   a. Divide 27 by $.05.
   b. Multiply $5.00 times 27.
   c. Multiply $.05 times 27.

3. Of the 27 stolen pencils, 13 were red, 13 were blue, and one was white. The red pencils are 7 inches long. The blue pencils are 8 inches long. And the white pencils are twice as long as the red pencils. How long was the stolen white pencil?

◆ What could you do to answer the question?
   a. Multiply 7 times 2.
   b. Multiply 8 times 2.
   c. Multiply 13 times 7.

4. Gina tracks down Lacy Eraser, a local pencil thief. Lacy admits to stealing the 27 pencils but says he doesn't have them anymore. Lacy says he split them up equally among his friends Inky, Smudge, and Leddy. How many pencils did each friend get?

◆ What could you do to answer the question?
a. Multiply 27 times 3.
b. Divide 27 by 3.
c. Subtract 3 from 27.

5. Gina tracks down the three friends and gets all the pencils back. It takes Gina 10 minutes to find Inky. It takes her three times as long to find Smudge. Gina finds Leddy in 15 minutes. What was the total time it took Gina to find the three friends?

◆ What could you do to answer the question?
a. Add 10, 3, and 15.
b. Multiply 10 times 3. Add 15 to that number.
c. Multiply 10 times 3. Add 10 and 15 to that number.

6. Now go back, and using your selections, answer each question.

Answer to number 1: _____

Answer to number 2: _____

Answer to number 3: _____

Answer to number 4: _____

Answer to number 5: _____

THINK IT OVER What are some ways to make sure you understand questions on school assignments?

Yard Work

Story Summary

Detective Carmen Chang uses area and perimeter to help put back some mixed-up lawns and fences.

The Questions

Students draw diagrams of yards and then figure out their area and perimeter.

Teaching Notes

It may seem that the real skill being taught here is computing area and perimeter (two very valuable lessons). However, the problem-solving strategy at work is "drawing a diagram." The problems can certainly be solved without drawing a diagram. But it is an excellent practice to visually represent a problem whenever possible. Students love to draw. It involves more senses in the problem-solving process. Seeing a problem makes it easier to grapple with.

Students can make simple sketches of the yards, making sure to label width and length. The diagrams could be drawn on graph paper, with each box representing a square foot. This will strongly reinforce the concept of "area": Students can count the number of boxes within the rectangle and see that it matches the number they found by multiplying the width and length.

In addition, scale diagrams of the yards will show that larger rectangles have larger areas.

◆ Yard Work ◆

It's not easy being Carmen Chang. It was the sunniest day of the summer. All the other kids were outside riding bikes, swimming, and playing baseball. But not me. I had to sit inside our dumb old office, waiting for the phone to ring. I looked out the window and dreamed I was at the beach. The sun shined. I took a sip from my cool iced tea. I listed to all the sounds of the beach: the wind, the ocean, the seagulls, the phone ringing...

Wait a minute! Why was the phone ringing at the beach? I snapped out of my dream and picked up the office phone. The voice on the phone said, "This is Moe D, Lonn. I need someone to meet me in my backyard. And hurry!"

Wow, a chance to go outside! I hung up the phone and rushed over to Mr. Lonn's house. He was standing in the yard. The grass came up to his belt!

"Maybe you should mow your lawn, mister," I said.

"I just mowed it yesterday!" said Moe.

"Grass really grows quickly around here,"
I answered.

"You don't understand. This isn't my yard! Someone stole my lawn!" Moe cried. He explained to me that someone had switched around the backyards on his street. Now the lawns and fences didn't fit right.

"This happened to everyone on your street?" I asked.

"Well, everybody except Rocky," said Moe.

So I went to the house of Rocky Ground. He was holding a shovel and was covered with grass clippings.

"Mr. Ground, do you know anything about the switched yards on this street?" I asked.

"Okay, okay, I did it!" said Rocky. "I can't grow anything in my yard. It's all dirt and stones. Everyone else has such pretty lawns. I was green with envy!"

"Well, Rocky, if you put everything back in the right place, I'm sure everyone will forgive you," I told him.

"I want to. But I can't remember which lawn and which fence goes where," said Rocky.

I told him I would help him by using area and perimeter. And that's how I caught another criminal red-handed. Okay, maybe it was green-handed.

NOW IT'S YOUR TURN...

Perimeter shows the distance around a shape. (A fence goes around the perimeter of a yard, for example.) To find the perimeter of a rectangle, you add the measurements of the four sides.

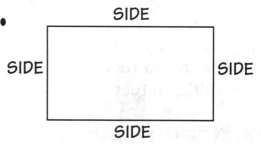

SIDE

SIDE   SIDE

SIDE

PERIMETER =
SIDE + SIDE + SIDE + SIDE

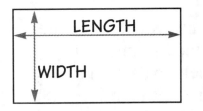

AREA = LENGTH x WIDTH

Area measures the space inside a shape. To find the area of a rectangle, you multiply the length times the width. We say the answer in "square units", such as square feet.

Perimeter is measured in units such as inches, feet and miles. Area is measured in "square units," such as square inches, square feet, and square miles. Imagine a square with a length of 1 inch and a width of 1 inch. The perimeter would be 1 inch + 1 inch + 1 inch + 1 inch, or 4 inches. The area would be 1 inch × 1 inch, or 1 "square inch."

A good way to understand area and perimeter is to draw a diagram of the rectangle. Be sure to label the length and the width.

Help Carmen find the area and perimeter of the yards on the street. The yards are all rectangles. The length and width of each yard is listed below. Draw a diagram of each one. Then find the area and perimeter.

1. Moe D. Lonn's yard
Length: 20 feet
Width: 15 feet

Perimeter: _____

Area: _____

2. Krissy Crabgrass's yard
Length: 15 feet
Width: 10 feet

Perimeter: _____

Area: _____

3. Rose Gardin's yard
Length: 30 feet
Width: 20 feet

Perimeter: _____

Area: _____

4. Jake Rake's yard
Length: 20 feet
Width: 12 feet

Perimeter: _____

Area: _____

5. Wade Weeder's yard
Length: 35 feet
Width: 17 feet

Perimeter: _____

Area: _____

6. Whose yard has the greatest...

a. perimeter? _____

b. area? _____

YOU CAN DO IT Use a ruler to find the length and width of this page. Then find the area and perimeter of the page.

THINK IT OVER What are some other reasons to know the area and perimeter of a yard?

Diving Into Mystery

Story Summary

Detective Chuck McBuck must look at suspects' attributes to determine who turned a swimming pool into a giant lemonade.

The Questions

Students compare attributes of different people to answer the questions.

Teaching Notes

Finding attributes helps students pay closer attention to the world around them. It is good practice for looking at similarities and differences in people, objects, places, words—anything. Students will begin to see how many different, detailed ways there are to describe things.

SKILL/STRATEGY

Finding attributes

Additional Skills:
◆ Comparing data
◆ Reading for detail

◆ Diving Into Mystery ◆

When you get invited to a pool, I'm sure you bring a towel, and maybe some suntan lotion and an inflatable duck. No such luck for Chuck McBuck. All I bring is my detective's notebook. Sure, everybody else has all the fun, while I'm solving crimes. But today I wasn't too upset. You see, it wasn't a great day for swimming at the Parklawn Community Pool. Unless you like swimming in lemonade.

When I arrived, I talked to Mark Spritz, the owner of the pool. He said that when he got to the pool that morning, he noticed something wasn't quite right.

"The giant ice cubes were the first thing I noticed," Mark said.

Mark figured that someone had dumped lemonade mix into the pool and stirred it up.

"The good news," said Mark, "is that we might have set a record for the world's largest drink."

"Now all you need," I added, "is the world's largest straw."

Mark didn't laugh.

"Are there any suspects?" I asked. "Who works here in the morning?"

"There are five people who could've committed this crime," said Mark.

He told me about his other morning employees. Frank N. Mustard runs the snack bar. C. P. Arr is the lifeguard. Wade Weeder is the gardener. Doreen Dryer hands out the towels. And Cloris Chlorine cleans the pool.

I didn't say anything to Mark, but I decided that he was also a suspect. I spoke to the other employees. Each one said they didn't do it.

"Yuck! I already have to look at lemonade all day long," said Frank, the snack bar guy.

"I would never put ice cubes in the water," said C. P., the lifeguard. "It's too dangerous."

"Lemonade mix?" said Wade, the gardener. "I would only use fresh lemons, right from the tree."

"I only like iced tea," said Doreen.

"My job is to clean the pool," said Cloris. "So why on Earth would I put lemonade mix in it?"

They all had good excuses. Just then I noticed a little boy standing outside the pool's gate. I walked toward him.

"When are they going to open the pool?" asked the boy.

"Not for a while," I said. "Who are you?"

"Zak Backstroke," the boy said. "I come here early every morning. I wait here at the gate until they open."

"Did you see someone dump lemonade mix into the pool this morning?" I asked.

"Yes, I did," said Zak. "I couldn't see the person's face. But it was a man with blond hair and a blue shirt."

"Thanks, Zak," I said. Now I could figure out who did it! A man with blond hair and a blue shirt—these were all "attributes." Attributes describe something. All I had to do was look at the attributes of the suspects. Whoever matched up to Zak's description made the giant lemonade!

Zak said it was a man. So it wasn't C. P., Doreen, or Cloris. That left three suspects: Mark, Frank, and Wade.

Zak also said the man had blond hair. Wade had brown hair. Two male suspects had blond hair: Mark and Frank.

The other thing Zak said was that the man was wearing a blue shirt. Frank's shirt was green. I looked at Mark, and noticed he was wearing a blue shirt! It must have been him!

"Mark, I figured out who did it," I said to Mr. Spritz. "It was you."

"Nice detective work, kid," said Mark. "I give up."

"Mark, you own the pool," I said. "Why would you want to ruin it?"

"I'm tired of running a pool," said Mark. "I've always dreamed of opening a nationwide chain of lemonade stands. To do that, you need an awful lot of lemonade."

Thanks to attributes, Mark's lemonade plans went sour. You could also say that his plans to ruin the community pool went down the drain.

NOW IT'S YOUR TURN...

Look at the pictures of the pool employees and read their lists of attributes to answer the following questions.

Attributes						
Name	Mark Spritz	Frank N. Mustard	Wade Weeder	C. P. Arr	Doreen Dryer	Cloris Chlorine
Hair	blond	blond	brown	red	blond	brown
Eyes	green	brown	blue	green	blue	brown
Shirt	blue	green	green	white	blue	white
Shorts	tan	blue	tan	red	red	blue
Height	6 ft, 1 in	5 ft, 8 in	6 ft	6 ft, 3 in	5 ft, 5 in	5 ft, 2 in

1. C. P. says that people should be at least 6 feet tall to go in the deep end of the pool. Which employee(s) could dive right in?

_____

2. Frank is having a special at the snack bar. Anyone with the same color hair and eyes gets a free bag of potato chips. Which employee(s) would get the chips?

_____

3. A voice comes out of the loudspeaker. "Would a person wearing something blue please report to the front desk." Which employee(s) would head to the desk?

_____

4. A huge crowd of people with blue clothes reports to the front desk. The loudspeaker speaks again. "Anyone with brown eyes can go back to the pool." Which employee(s) would stay at the front desk?

_____

5. The pool's "Employee of the Month" has a first name and last name that both start with the same letter.

   a. Who might it be? _____

   b. The first and last names also have the letter "D" in them. Now who's left?_____

   c. The person is wearing red shorts today. Who is it? _____

YOU CAN DO IT Make a list of attributes about yourself. Which attributes do you share with other people in the class?

Estimation Celebration

Story Summary

Detective Cesar Hidalgo uses estimation to decide how many supplies to get for the agency's party.

The Questions

Students estimate the necessary number of several party items.

Teaching Notes

Making an estimate is not only a very important consumer skill. Students may not realize how widespread the use of estimates is. Bring in newspaper articles. Have students circle numbers in articles. Then try to figure out which are exact numbers, and which are estimates. Words like "about," "more than," "less than," and "approximately" usually accompany estimates in print. Have students discuss why they think estimates were used in these instances.

SKILL/STRATEGY

Making an estimate

Additional Skills:
◆ Whole number $\times$, $\div$
◆ Working with money
◆ Critical thinking

Name _____

◆ Estimation Celebration ◆

Everyone here at the Effective Detective Agency is pretty sharp. But when there's a really tough case, they always come to me. I'm Cesar Hidalgo. That's why I was handed the trickiest assignment of the year: buying food for our annual party.

"Okay, everybody," I announced to my fellow detectives. "I need to know who's coming to this party."

"Let's see," said Gina. "My cousins, Lila and Mila, are visiting that day, so I have to bring them. My friend Ted likes Mila, so I have to invite him. And if Ted goes, Jill will want to come."

Chuck interrupted. "Jill lives next door to my pal Rosie, so we have to invite her. Rosie never goes anywhere without Lewis. Lewis will probably have to bring his kid sister Alice. She'll want someone to play with, so I'll bring my brother Frankie."

"The party might not fit in the office," said Carmen. "We could rent a giant tent and set it up in the park. I think we have to get permission from the city, but Cesar can do that. Then, if we have the party outdoors, we can bring our pets! But if it rains, we might have to rent the gym, too."

"This sounds cool!" said Tommy. "If it's going to be a big party, we'll need music. I'll call my Uncle Carl, who runs Carl's All-Tuba Orchestra."

"Hold it! Hold it! Hold it!" I screamed. "We're not having any tents, pets, or tubas! Each of us is allowed to invite 3 guests, and that's all!" I didn't want to be mean, but sometimes you have to lay down some rules with this bunch.

A few days later, I was looking over the list of guests. I studied it as closely as I would study a list of suspects. I would have to secretly follow each person, to figure out how much food I needed to get. How many hamburgers would each person eat? What if some of the guests didn't come? What if some extra people snuck in? What if some people don't like hamburgers? The pressure was too much!

"Gina, I give up," I said with a sad look on my face. "I can't figure out how much food to get. It's too much work."

Gina patted me on the back. "Don't worry, Just use estimation. You don't need to know exactly how much food to get—you **just need** a good guess. Estimation can help you."

"Gina, I'll make you my assistant party planner if you tell me more about estimation."

"Sure thing, Cesar. How many people are coming?"

"Hmmm," I said. "Five detectives invited 3 people each. Five times 3 equals 15, so there are 15 guests. Fifteen guests plus the 5 detectives equals 20 people."

"Okay, let's say each person will eat 2 hamburgers," said Gina. "Some will eat more, and some will eat less, but 2 hamburgers each is a good guess. Twenty times 2 equals 40. You should buy 40 hamburgers."

"I get it now," I said. "With estimation, you'll never buy way too much stuff, or way too little. I can use estimation to figure out how much of everything I need to buy. Now there's only one mystery left."

"What's that, Cesar?" Gina asked.

"How am I going to carry all this stuff back from the supermarket?"

NOW IT'S YOUR TURN...

Use estimation to answer the questions.

1. Cesar estimated that each of the 20 people at the party would drink 3 cans of soda.

   a. How many cans will he need to buy? _____

   b. Soda comes in packages of 6 cans.

    How many packages will Cesar have to buy? _____

2. Say Cesar let all 5 detectives invite 4 friends each to the party. He estimates that everyone will eat 2 hamburgers each.

   How many hamburgers should he buy? _____

3. Estimate how many of the following items each party guest would use. Then figure out how many of each Cesar should buy for the party (based on 20 people attending).

a. Hot dogs _____

b. Cups _____

c. Napkins _____

d. Slices of pizza _____

e. Bags of potato chips _____

4. How could Cesar use estimation to figure out how much money he'll need at the supermarket? Explain your answer.

_____

_____

_____

_____

_____

5. Plan a party for your class! Make a list of everything you'd need to buy. Count how many people are in your class. Then use estimation to figure out how much of each item you'll need to get.

THINK IT OVER Estimation helps you make good guesses about numbers. When are some times when you would need to know the exact number of things, instead of an estimate?

Too Much Talking!

Story Summary

Detective Gina Jasper questions a person who's giving her too much information.

The Questions

Students pick out the necessary facts in word problems and then solve them.

Teaching Notes

Understanding a word problem and solving it can be difficult enough. The following problems raise the stakes a bit by providing too much information. The questions are loaded with numbers that have nothing to do with the problem. Students must read carefully, decide what information is crucial, and correctly solve the problem. This is an important real-world skill, especially in a time where we are often bombarded with information. Knowing what is relevant can make all the difference. Before students read the story, discuss with them the importance of looking for necessary information whenever they read.

SKILL/STRATEGY

"Too Much Information" problems

Additional Skills:
- ◆ Reading for detail
- ◆ Whole number +, −, ×, ÷
- ◆ Money ÷
- ◆ Computing with time
- ◆ Critical thinking

◆ Too Much Talking! ◆

Gina Jasper here. Being a detective is tough for some of the other kids, but not for me. Sometimes I think I can read minds or something. It makes my work a snap. For example, I walked into our office the other day. A girl was pacing back and forth. She looked nervous. Somehow I knew that she had been the victim of a robbery.

"Let me guess," I said to the girl. "Someone stole something from you."

"That's right," said the girl. "How did you know that?"

"It's hard to explain," I explained. "When you're a top-notch detective like me, you just know. So who are you?"

The girl stopped pacing. "My name is Gabby Tock. I'm 10 years old. Actually, I'm 9 years, 11 months old. But I tell people that I'm 10. Because soon I will be 10,

 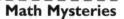

and I don't want them to think I'm 9. We're going to have a big birthday party. We'll have a chocolate cake. Chocolate is my favorite flavor. Strawberry is good, too, but not as good as chocolate. The party will be on a Saturday. My birthday is really on the Thursday before that. My mom thinks more people will come if it's on Saturday. On Saturday I'll be 10 years and 2 days old. We might have a special dinner on Thursday, with chicken and potatoes and—"

"Yes, yes, that's very interesting," I said, before Gabby could say another word. "But what I really want to know about is the robbery. What was stolen?"

"Oh, you want to know about the robbery. I'll tell you all about it," Gabby said. "Is it okay if I sit down?" Gabby sat down. "Sometimes I like to stand, but other times I like to sit. We might play musical chairs at my party! This is a nice chair. I like chairs made out of wood. They're better than metal chairs or plastic chairs. My dad has a favorite chair. He likes to read the newspaper in his favorite chair when he comes home from work. Sometimes, Ralph is in the chair when Dad gets home. Ralph is our dog. Here's a picture of my family and Ralph." Gabby held up a picture. "Ralph's funny! If he sees another dog across the street, he'll bark and bark and bark! But if the dog comes close to

Ralph, then Ralph gets real scared. Anyway, if Dad finds Ralph in his chair, Dad yells at Ralph. Dad's face gets red when he yells. One time Ralph was chewing Dad's newspaper, and my mom came into the—"

I stopped Gabby again. "Gabby, I'm sure this is a great story. But you were about to tell me what was stolen."

Gabby held her hands to her cheeks. "How silly of me! I'm sorry. My diary was stolen. It's a really nice diary. It has a big lock on it. There are pictures of horses and stars all over the front and back of the diary. Horses are my most favorite kind of animal. I asked my dad if we could get a horse. He told me Ralph wouldn't like that. But he said someday, if I'm good, we can go ride horses. It would probably hurt if you fell off a horse. But I would be really careful. I would ride it slowly, so I wouldn't—"

This girl could really talk! "Gabby, I love horses, too. But you're giving me too much information. You need to tell me about the robbery. I need to know about the stolen diary."

"Oh, that? My little brother stole the diary. But he gave it back."

Now I was mad. "Gabby, you know who took the diary? And you got it back? Then why did you come to a detective agency for help?"

Gabby gave me a strange look. "I didn't come for help. I just need to use the bathroom. Where is it?"

I pointed down the hall. "Third door on the left."

Gabby walked down the hall. I guess my mind-reading powers aren't perfect yet. That's okay. I'm still young.

NOW IT'S YOUR TURN...

Just like Gabby, sometimes math problems give you too much information. Read the following problems, and the question for each one. Underline the facts you'll need to answer the question. Solve the problem and write the answer in the blank.

1. Gabby was in the bathroom for 14 minutes. She left the faucet on for 8 minutes, but the plug was in the drain. So 15 gallons of water spilled onto the floor! Gabby pulled 38 paper towels off the rack to wipe up the spill. Gabby tried to sneak out the back door before anyone noticed. It took her 11 minutes to find the exit. How many minutes was Gabby in the bathroom with the faucet off?

_____

2. Gabby wrote about her day in her diary. She started writing at 4:33 P.M. By 5:10 she had written 36 pages. On half the pages, she drew pictures of horses. On 13 other pages, she drew 11 pictures of cats, and 6 pictures of flowers. Gabby's dad called her down for dinner at 5:47. How many pages had pictures of horses?

_____

3. Gina was tired after Gabby's visit. She tried to take a nap. Gina put 6 pillows under her head. Four of the pillows were blue, and 2 were yellow. Gina slept for 26 minutes. She had a dream that was 9 minutes long. In the dream, Gina was chased by 12 girls who looked like Gabby, 8 men who looked like Gabby's dad, and 14 boys who looked like Gabby's brother. They were all talking nonstop! They chased Gina for 37 miles. How many people were chasing Gina?

_____

 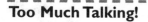

4. Gabby's dog Ralph is 6 years old. He dug 14 holes in the backyard. He dropped 3 bones into each hole. Ralph chewed up Gabby's dad's newspaper and dropped it in 8 of the holes. Gabby's dad walked down the 4 steps into the backyard. He saw what Ralph did and yelled for 16 minutes. What is the total number of bones Ralph dropped into the holes?

_____

5. It takes Gabby's dad 32 minutes to get home on bus number 17. Before he gets on the bus, Gabby's dad buys 6 copies of the newspaper. He plans to give 5 papers to Ralph, and still have one to read. The total cost of the newspapers is $3.00. When Gabby's dad walks in the front door, he trips on 46 marbles. Half of the marbles are black. While Dad is on the floor, Ralph chews up all 6 newspapers. How much does one newspaper cost?

_____

YOU CAN DO IT Write your own "too much information" problem starring Gabby and her family. Exchange problems with your classmates and solve the problems.

THINK IT OVER Why do think it's a good idea to underline the important facts in each problem?

Watch Your Step!

Story Summary

Detective Tommy Tompkins tries to prove that Lou and Drew Toostepp stole a pie.

The Questions

Students decide which two math operations are needed to solve word problems and then determine the answer.

Teaching Notes

Two-step problems are an introduction to a concept students will face the rest of their lives: multistep problems. Rather than rushing to find solutions to the problems, students will have to first recognize that there are two steps to be completed. Students employ the rational thinking that comes up so often in mathematics and in life: One step must be solved first, and then the other.

Students should be reminded that they may not all use the same two steps to solve the problems. For example, a problem that says "1/2 of the 8 hats" could be solved with division ($8 \div 2$). However, a student familiar with fraction multiplication might solve it another way ($8 \times 1/2$).

Name _____

◆ Watch Your Step! ◆

The phone rang twice before I picked it up.

"Hello, can I help you?" I asked into the phone.

"Where's my pie? I am so hungry!" said the voice on the other end.

"Mister, you've got the wrong number," I said. "This is the Effective Detective Agency, not Vito's Pizza World."

"No, no, not pizza pie—blueberry pie," said the voice. "My name is Roscoe Rhodes, and I need a detective to find my stolen pie."

"Then you did call the right place," I said. "I'm Detective Tommy Tompkins, and I'll be right over."

Mr. and Mrs. Rhodes were waiting in their kitchen for me. Mrs. Rhodes pointed at the windowsill. "We baked a pie this morning. I told Roscoe not to let it cool on the windowsill. It could fall right off."

Mr. Rhodes spoke up. "It cools best on the windowsill. Besides, I was keeping an eye on it while I mowed the lawn. But when I came back inside, the pie was gone."

 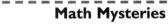

I told Mr. and Mrs. Rhodes that I needed to investigate. The windowsill was too high off the ground for a person to reach. Then I noticed two sets of footprints going across the freshly mowed lawn. The footprints went from the sidewalk to the window and then back to the sidewalk. Finally, I saw the most important clue: There was only one set of footprints directly in front of the window.

I had a hunch about the case. I went to the nearby house of Lou and Drew Toostepp. I had caught these twin brothers stealing baked goods before. This case seemed to fit the pattern.

"What's the problem, Tommy?" the twins asked at the same time.

"I think you boys stole Mr. and Mrs. Rhodes's blueberry pie," I said.

"Prove it!" they said.

"OK, I will." I told them my theory. "There were two sets of footprints across the lawn. You two always work together, so I think they're your footprints."

"We couldn't steal that pie," said the twins. "The Rhodes's windowsill is too high for us to reach."

"Exactly," I said. "That's why there's only one set of footprints in front of the window. One of you climbed on the other's shoulders and grabbed the pie."

"Nice theory, Tommy," said Lou and Drew. "But do you have any real evidence?"

"Yes, I do." I pointed at the twins. "Your mouths are covered with blueberry pie."

After that, the twins admitted to the crime. I ordered them to replace the Rhodes's blueberry pie. Looks like this time, Lou and Drew really "blue" it!

NOW IT'S YOUR TURN...

Wherever Lou and Drew go, you'll see two sets of footsteps. In the following problems, you'll see two math steps. Decide which two steps you'll need to answer each question. Write a math sign (+, −, ×, or ÷) in each blank. (You may use the same operation twice.) Then find the answer to each question. We'll show you how in the first problem.

1. In Tommy's investigation, he found 24 sets of Lou and Drew's footprints leading from the sidewalk to the window. He found 28 more leading away from the window. Tommy also found bigger footprints belonging to Mr. Rhodes. There were 17 less sets of Mr. Rhodes' footprints than all of Lou and Drew's sets combined. How many sets of footprints did Mr. Rhodes leave on the lawn?

First, we have to find the two math steps. The question asks how many sets of footprints Mr. Rhodes left. The problem says he left 17 less sets than all of Lou and Drew's sets. So first we have to add together all of Lou and Drew's sets of footprints. Then we'll have to subtract 17 to find out how many sets Mr. Rhodes left. So our two math steps are addition and subtraction (+ and −).

Next, we find the answer. In our first step, we use addition to add together all of Lou and Drew's sets of footprints (24 and 28). We know 24 + 28 = 52. So Lou and Drew left 52 sets of footprints.

In our second step, we subtract 17 from 52, because Mr. Rhodes left 17 sets less than Lou and Drew. We know 52 − 17 = 35. So Mr. Rhodes left 35 sets of footprints.

Two Steps: _____ 24 + 28 _____ and _____ 52 − 17 _____

Answer: _ 35 sets of footprints _____

2. Mr. and Mrs. Rhodes made 10 blueberry pies this month. They made twice as many apple pies. How many pies did they make all together?

Two Steps: _____ and _____

Answer: _____

3. Mr. Rhodes spent 44 minutes making the blueberry pie. He spent half as long mowing the lawn. Mr. Rhodes cried for 15 minutes more than he mowed the lawn when he found out the pie was gone. How many minutes did Mr. Rhodes cry?

Two Steps: _____ and _____

Answer: _____

4. It cost Lou and Drew $7.50 to buy a new blueberry pie for the Rhodes. They also bought a box of donuts, which cost $4.22 less than the pie. Then Lou and Drew bought a jumbo cookie that cost $2.17 less than the donuts. How much did the cookie cost?

Two Steps: _____ and _____

Answer: _____

5. Tommy is so hungry when he gets home, he orders a super-size pizza from Vito's Pizza World. He munches 8 slices right away. Gina comes by and eats $1/4$ the number of slices that Tommy ate. How many more slices did Tommy eat than Gina?

Two Steps: _____ and _____

Answer: _____

Good Buys for Spies

Story Summary

Detectives Carmen Chang and Tommy Tompkins read a display to find out the prices of the wacky items at Sly's Spy Shop.

The Questions

Students read a display and compute with money to figure out the costs of various purchases.

Teaching Notes

Reading a display is a crucial consumer skill that helps solve many real-life problems. Think how many times you've stared at a price display at a snack bar and had to quickly figure out "Can I afford the items I want?" An interesting element of these problems is that all the information needed to find the solution is not included within the problem. Students must go outside the problem, locate the necessary data on the display, and then begin to solve.

SKILL/STRATEGY
Reading a display
Additional Skills: ◆ Money +, −, ×, ÷ ◆ Guess and check ◆ Reading for detail

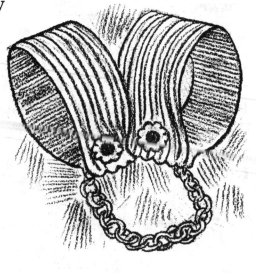

◆ Good Buys for Spies ◆

In the detective business, it's important to keep up with the times. You can't just rely on your wits anymore. All the bad guys out there are piling up the latest computerized equipment. We have to match them every step of the way. That's why, once a year, the Effective Detective Agency takes a trip to Sly's Spy Shop. Sly, the Spy Guy, carries a complete line of the most up-to-date crime-fighting gadgets. This year, Tommy and I dropped by Sly's place to pick up a few items.

"Wow, look at all this cool stuff!" said Tommy, as soon as we walked in the door. Here's some of the things we saw:

◆ **The Finger Stinger Automatic Fingerprint Reader:** The Stinger sends the fingerprint readouts into a computer database. The computer is hooked up to glove stores around the world. If those hands tried on a pair of gloves in the last five years, the computer can catch them red-handed. Or red-glove-handed.

- **The Non-Phony Phone:** Crooks expect detectives to have cleverly disguised phones. Phones that look like shoes. Phones that look like footballs. Phones that look like cantaloupes. This phone actually looks like a phone. It fools them every time.

- **Fake Chin:** The fake beard is a very popular disguise. But what if the detective already has a beard? Or what if a detective is wearing a fake beard and needs to be disguised again? The Fake Chin is the answer. With a few drops of glue, it makes your chin look clean shaven.

- **Magnifying Drinking Glass:** Being a detective can be tiring work. Sometimes, when you're hot on the trail of a thief, you get really hot. But you don't have time to stop for a refreshing cool drink. This handy drinking glass solves the problem. It works like a normal glass. But the clear bottom is actually a high-powered magnifying glass. Cool down without slowing down!

- **Nose for Crime:** Every criminal has a different smell. The nose knows! This computerized nose sniffs out the crime scene. It figures out who the criminal is. Then, **a** detailed fact sheet about the criminal is printed out on a tissue. It comes out the left nostril. You'll never "blow" a case again!

- **Handsome Handcuffs:** Crooks don't like to wear even the most comfortable handcuffs. That's because they're silly looking. Well, those days are over. New Handsome Handcuffs come in a variety of styles and colors. They'll match any outfit a crook is wearing.

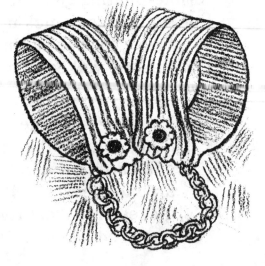

Thieves will beg you to catch them, just so they can wear these stylish cuffs!

- **Snakers:** Getting to the crime scene in a hurry is always tough. But you'd sure get there quick if you were being chased by two snakes, right? That's why we've created Snakers, the snake sneakers. Our patented Fake Snake is glued to the back of each shoe. They're so real looking, you'll forget they're fake! You'll be sure to keep criminals on the run with these great shoes.

- **Super-Duper Top-Secret World-Class First-Rate Security Alarm:** This is the world's finest alarm system. It was created with technology so top secret, we cannot even talk about it. But trust us, it will stop every criminal every time. Only one available per store. Ask clerk for a demonstration.

After we looked at all the items, we went to talk to Sly, the owner. It was hard to find him, because he was dressed up as a vacuum.

"Pretty nice disguise, huh?" said the vacuum.

"You tricked us again, Sly," I said. "Hey, how much does everything cost? There weren't any price tags on the merchandise."

"I've got a new system," said the vacuum. "All the prices are listed on that giant display. As I always say, my prices are a real steal!" The vacuum laughed and pointed to the big sign.

"Hey, could we see a demonstration of that super-duper alarm system?" I asked.

"I'm sorry," said the vacuum. I can't show it to you."

"Why not?" asked Tommy.

"You won't believe this," said the vacuum. "But somebody stole it."

NOW IT'S YOUR TURN...

Read the price display to answer the questions.

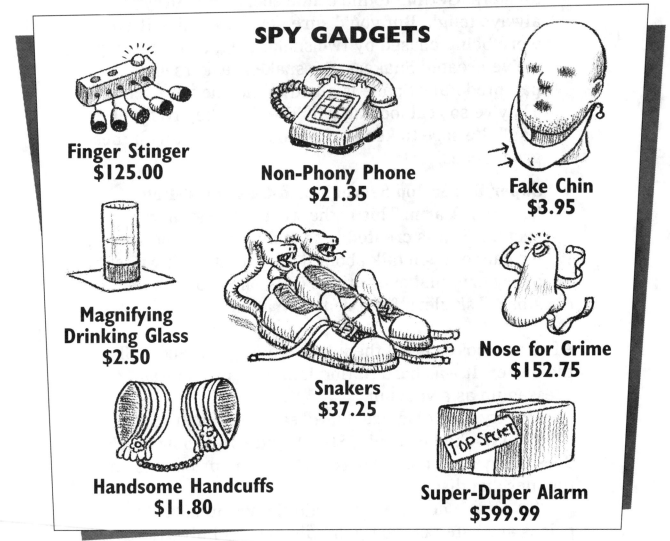

SPY GADGETS

Finger Stinger
$125.00

Non-Phony Phone
$21.35

Fake Chin
$3.95

Magnifying Drinking Glass
$2.50

Snakers
$37.25

Nose for Crime
$152.75

Handsome Handcuffs
$11.80

Super-Duper Alarm
$599.99

1. Tommy wants to buy the Handsome Handcuffs and a Fake Chin. How much will he spend in all?

_____

2. Carmen wants to buy Magnifying Drinking Glasses for all 5 detectives at the agency. What will be the total cost of the glasses?

_____

3. A secret agent brought exactly enough money to buy the Super-Duper Alarm. It's not available, so the agent decides to buy Finger Stingers instead. How many Stingers can the agent afford?

_____

4. Agent 0017, James Blond, decides to buy the Nose for Crime, a Non-Phony Phone, and a pair of Snakers. How much will he spend?

_____

5. Carmen can't afford the Super-Duper Alarm, so she makes her own out of a bucket, some bells, Scotch tape, and a gallon of milk. She spends $7.45 on her alarm, which she calls "Alarmin' Carmen." How much money did she save, compared to buying the Super-Duper Alarm?

_____

6. The Young Detectives' Society gives the Effective Detective Agency a $100 gift certificate for Sly's Spy Shop. Come up with three different lists of items they could buy with $100.

a. _____

b. _____

c. _____

YOU CAN DO IT Come up with your own crime-fighting devices. Write advertisements for the items. Don't forget about the prices!

Duck, Duck, Loose!

Story Summary

Detective Cesar Hidalgo is hot on the trail of a duck thief. But he must track down missing information before catching the crook.

The Questions

Students determine what information is missing from some word problems. They make up a fact to complete the problem and then answer the question.

Teaching Notes

"Too Little Information" problems are a close relative of "Too Much Information" problems. This time around, vital numbers are missing, making it impossible to answer the stated questions. These are open-ended problems, allowing students to make up their own facts so they can answer the questions. As long as their fact allows them to answer the question, they are correct. Encourage creative responses! (Though outrageously large numbers will make computation a bit tougher!)

◆ Duck, Duck, Loose! ◆

If you don't like ducks, don't go to Down Street. There used to be a store on Down Street called Danny's Downtown Ducks. It was a pet store that sold only—you guessed it—ducks. No dogs, no cats, no birds, no fish. Just ducks. The store closed a few years ago, but it left its mark. Everyone who lives on Down Street has a house full of ducks. That's why I wasn't surprised when I got some strange phone calls the other day.

"This is Cesar at Effective Detective Agency. How can I help you?" I said into the phone.

"This is Mrs. Feathers at 14 Down Street. Somebody stole 11 of my ducks," said the first caller.

Then there was another call. "Hey, this is Bill, from 15 Down Street," said the second caller. "I'm missing 13 ducks."

Finally, there was a third call. "I'm Mal Lard from 16 Down Street," said the voice.

"Let me guess," I said. "Somebody stole your goose." It sounded like a classic "duck, duck, goose" robbery.

"Close," said Mal. "Somebody swiped my ducks."

"I'm coming down to Down Street to solve the case," I said.

Down Street was very quiet when I got there. Actually, it wasn't that quiet. There was an awful lot of quacking. Then I noticed something odd—a man walking down the street, followed by a line of 36 ducks. He looked like the Pied Piper! The Pied Piper of ducks, anyway. Suddenly I recognized the man. It was Danny, the former owner of Danny's Downtown Ducks.

"Hey, Danny," I called out. "Where did you get all those ducks?"

Danny turned around. "Hi, Cesar. Haven't seen you in a while. What ducks are you talking about?" He looked behind him. "Oh, you mean these ducks! I don't know. I guess they're just following me. Ducks like me very much."

"That's a good story, Danny," I said. "But I think you stole those ducks from Mrs. Feathers, Bill, and Mal Lard."

"Prove it," said Danny.

Now I was a little angry. "I will. You've got 36 ducks with you. Well, Mrs. Feathers is missing 11 ducks. Bill is missing 13 ducks. And Mal Lard is missing…" Whoops! I forgot to ask Mal Lard how many of his ducks were

stolen. I didn't have enough information! "I'll be right back," I said to Danny.

I hurried to Mal's house at 16 Down Street. Mal told me he was missing 12 ducks. I rushed back to Danny. He hadn't gotten too far away. Ducks walk pretty slowly.

"Ah-ha! Mal is missing 12 ducks," I yelled. "To find the total number of missing ducks, I'll just add 11, 12, and 13. That equals 36 ducks. Which is the exact number of ducks following you, Danny."

Danny admitted to the crime and promised to return the ducks. And that's how I quacked, uh, cracked the case.

NOW IT'S YOUR TURN...

Just like in Cesar's duck search, each of the following problems is missing some information. Read each one and figure out what important information is missing. Then make up a fact that will let you answer the question. Solve each problem using the information you made up. We'll show you how in the first problem.

1. Mal's other ducks were all crying while their 12 friends were gone. Luckily, their feathers were waterproof. How many ducks were still in the house with Mal?

To solve the problem, you need to subtract the 12 missing ducks from the number of ducks Mal has all together. But the problem doesn't say how many ducks Mal owns! So you need to make up that fact. Say Mal had 25 ducks all together. Now we just subtract 12 from 25. We know that 25 − 12 = 13. So 13 ducks were still in the house with Mal.

My Made-Up Fact: _Mal had 25 ducks all together._

Answer: _13 ducks_

2. Danny didn't get too far with those ducks. But at least he traveled 3 times farther than the last thief on Down Street, Snyder the Sneaky Snail Bandit. How far did Danny get?

My Made-Up Fact: _____

_____

Answer: _____

3. Mrs. Feathers went to Pedro's Pet Store to buy another bird. There was a very nice ostrich. Pedro said he would charge Mrs. Feathers $1 per pound for the bird. But then Mrs. Feathers saw a penguin that cost $10 more than the ostrich. How much did the penguin cost?

My Made-Up Fact: _____

_____

Answer: _____

4. After Danny returned the ducks, Bill checked his closely to make sure they were okay. Four of Bill's most nervous ducks had lost some feathers! Four feathers fell off Chip's left wing. Skip was missing 7 feathers. Bip had lost 6 times more feathers than Flip. What was the total number of feathers missing from Chip, Skip, Bip, and Flip?

My Made-Up Fact: _____

_____

Answer: _____

5. Cesar decided to make sure all the ducks were safe at home. He started checking at 4:00 P.M. Fifteen minutes later, he was done at Bill's house and left for Mrs. Feather's place. It took 2 minutes to walk from Mrs. Feather's house to Mal Lard's door. At what time did Cesar arrive at Mal's house?

My Made-Up Fact: _____

_____

Answer: _____

6. Cesar was walking home down Down Street. He heard a boy yell out, "Duck!" Cesar thought it was nice that a boy was talking to a duck. Then Cesar got hit in the head with a Frisbee. "I told you to duck," said the boy.

Cesar sat on the curb, and rubbed the bump on his head. While he was sitting, a baby duck made a nest in his hair. The baby duck was half as tall as the bump on Cesar's head. How tall was the baby duck?

My Made-Up Fact: _____

_____

_____

Answer: _____

YOU CAN DO IT Make up your own "missing information" problem about the ducks on Down Street. Trade problems with a classmate!

Tree Trouble

Story Summary

Detective Chuck McBuck draws tree diagrams to count his disguises before catching a mysterious branch chopper.

The Questions

Students draw tree diagrams to find the number of disguise combinations the detectives can wear for a variety of cases.

Teaching Notes

Tree diagrams allow us to visualize problems involving combinations. Without a knowledge of the basics of combinatorics (which this lesson could serve as an introduction to), there is no simple way to know all possible combinations, given a certain number of elements. Most people would start randomly listing combinations. This often leads to duplicating combinations and leaving out combinations. It is a time-consuming and inaccurate process. Tree diagrams are a much more efficient, reliable method.

You may want to have a class discussion on other uses of tree diagrams (family trees, sports tournament brackets, etc.).

◆ Tree Trouble ◆

Autumn is my favorite time of year. I love to watch the leaves fall from the trees. That's why they call it "fall," you know. It's nice to walk down the street and see all the trees without any leaves. But it wasn't so nice to walk down Maple Lane and see trees without any branches!

"What happened to these trees?" I asked a man walking down the street.

"These trees?" said the man. "They started out as acorns. Then, with a lot of sunlight and water, young trees grew. After years and years, they got taller, thicker, and stronger."

"Yes, yes," I said. " I know how trees grow. I want to know what happened to the branches!"

The man looked up at the trees. "Yikes! Someone cut off all the branches! This is a mystery!"

Whenever there's a mystery, I'm the only person you need—Detective Chuck McBuck. I raced back to the offices of the Effective Detective Agency.

Sure enough, we had received several calls reporting branch choppings all over town. I was furious! Who could possibly be so cruel to the environment? I had to catch this mad chopper, no matter how long it took.

I decided to hide out in our town's parks until I caught this person. Like any great detective, I would have to wear disguises. But how many disguises could I wear?

I searched through my desk, and found all my disguise items. I had two hats: a chef's hat and a Viking helmet. I had two wigs: a curly red wig and a spiky blue wig. I also had two pairs of glasses: black sunglasses and shop-class safety goggles.

I could figure out the possible disguise combinations by making "tree diagrams." I matched up my chef's hat with each wig and pair of glasses with this diagram:

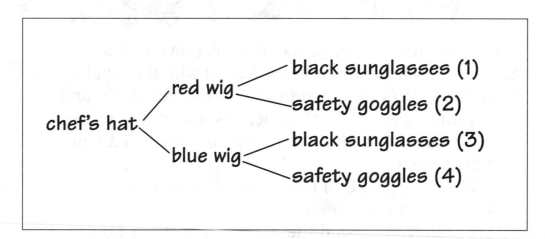

Now I knew there were 4 different disguise combinations for each hat I had. Since I had 2 hats, I could make 2 times 4, or 8 different disguise combinations.

I went from park to park with my disguises. I caught the chopper while wearing disguise number 7: a Viking helmet, spiky blue wig, and black sunglasses.

"Oh, it's you, McBuck," said Arbor Barber, the branch chopper. "You never would have caught me without that clever disguise. Now I won't be able to bring these branches back to my branch office."

"You're in a lot of trouble now," I said. "But tell me one thing: Why were you stealing all these branches?"

Arbor Barber smiled. "I was going to roast some really big marshmallows."

The town's trees were safe once again. My tree diagrams did a "tree-mendous" job!

NOW IT'S YOUR TURN...

Here's a list of disguise items from the Effective Detective Agency. Use it to make tree diagrams to solve the following problems.

HATS	WIGS	GLASSES	SHOES	OUTFITS
chef's hat	red wig	sunglasses	clown shoes	tuxedo
Viking helmet	blue wig	safety goggles	snowshoes	wedding dress
baseball cap	bald wig	X-ray specs	cowboy boots	chicken suit
top hat			high heels	
hard hat				

1. Gina is trying to catch a rice thief at a wedding. She decides to wear either a wedding dress or tuxedo and a wig (but no other items). How many disguise combinations can she wear for the case?

2. Someone is putting oatmeal into wet cement. Cesar goes undercover as a construction worker. He decides to wear a hard hat, the red or blue wig, and a pair of glasses. How many disguise combinations can he wear for the case?

3. Someone stole the recipe for peanut butter and jelly sandwiches from Roger's Restaurant. Chuck decides to wear a chef's hat, sunglasses or X-ray specs, and a pair of shoes. How many disguise combinations can he wear for the case?

4. Someone's been giving Farmer Joe's chickens really bad haircuts. Carmen decides to wear the chicken suit, the bald wig, and a pair of shoes. How many disguise combinations can she wear for the case?

5. The sail of the S.S. Esmerelda has been replaced with Captain Meano's pajamas! For the case, Tommy decides to wear the Viking helmet, the tuxedo, a wig, and some glasses. How many disguise combinations can he wear for the case?

6. Someone stole Cowboy Charlie's favorite piece of chewing gum. Cesar pulls out the cowboy boots, the red and blue wigs, the glasses, and the hats. How many disguise combinations can he wear for the case?

YOU CAN DO IT Make up some more zany disguise items. Then make tree diagrams to show how many combinations you could wear.

A Slippery Case

Story Summary

Detective Gina Jasper uses a logic box to find out who stole a golden banana from Vanna's Banana Land.

The Questions

Students make and complete logic boxes to sort out information in word problems.

SKILL/STRATEGY

Using a logic box

Additional Skill:
◆ Reading for detail

Teaching Notes

A logic box is a handy way to organize information. It is a clear, visual representation of data. In these problems, logic boxes match people (listed in the left column) to details (listed across the top).

The provided clues tell students whether or not the people match the various details. "Yes" or "No" is written in the corresponding squares. (This also reinforces coordinate graphing skills: Finding the point where a certain row meets a certain column.) By a simple process of elimination, students will be able to fill in the entire box based on only a few clues.

	Detail X	Detail Y	Detail Z
Person A			
Person B			
Person C			

When students are comfortable with logic box problems, have them take another look at "Diving Into Mystery" (page 29). Ask them if they can solve the mystery presented in the story by using a logic box, instead of "finding attributes." Afterward, discuss which problem-solving method worked better for the mystery.

◆ A Slippery Case ◆

My name is Gina Jasper. Vanna Vandanna called me today at the Effective Detective Agency. Ms. Vandanna runs Vanna's Banana Land.

"Someone stole my banana!" Vanna cried.

"So what? You've got a store full of bananas," I said.

"You don't understand. This was a golden banana," answered Vanna.

"It'll be brown in a couple of days. That's how bananas work, Ms. Vandanna," I explained.

"You still don't understand," replied Vanna. "The banana was made of gold."

I told Vanna I'd be right over. It sounded like an a-"peel"ing case.

A few minutes later, I arrived at Banana Land. Vanna was waiting for me, holding an empty banana peel.

Vanna told me what happened. "That golden banana is worth a lot of money. That's why I hide it in a real peel. I always keep it in my desk in the back room.

When I came back from lunch today, the banana was gone."

She said that only four of her workers are allowed in that room—Connie, Bonnie, Donny, and Ronny. Old Man Nichols, the guard, makes sure no one else goes in. Vanna said that Mr. Nichols was a good guard but sometimes got a little confused. I decided to talk to him.

"Mr. Nichols, we're in a pickle," I said.

"Pickle? There are no pickles here. Only bananas," Nichols said.

I asked Mr. Nichols if he saw the robbery.

"Yes, I did," he said. "Someone walked out of that room holding the golden banana. The person was wearing a red hat, yellow shirt, and blue pants."

"Why didn't you catch the thief, Mr. Nichols?" I asked.

"I fell asleep," he said.

"Okay," I said, "was the thief Connie, Bonnie, Donny, or Ronny?"

Old Man Nichols scratched his head. "It was one of those. They all look the same to me, actually."

I could still solve the case, using a little trick called a "logic box." First, I did a little detective work, and found out these clues:

☞ Bonnie and Connie wore red baseball caps today. Ronny didn't wear a hat. Donny was wearing a red cap.

☞ Bonnie wore a white shirt to work today. Connie, Donny, and Ronny all wore their yellow "Banana Land" shirts.

☞ Connie wore a black skirt today. Bonnie and Donny wore blue jeans. Ronny wore white shorts.

Next I drew a logic box. I wrote the names of the suspects down the left side. I wrote the clues across the top.

	red hat	yellow shirt	blue pants
Bonnie			
Connie			
Donny			
Ronny			

Help me solve the case by filling in the logic box. See if each suspect fits each clue. Write "Yes" in a box under a clue next to a person's name if it's true. Write "No" in the box if it's not true. The person who has a "Yes" under every clue is the thief.

1. Now tell me: Who is the slippery banana thief?

_____

NOW IT'S YOUR TURN...

The following logic boxes are slightly different. There is one, and only one, "Yes" in every row and column. So if after reading a clue, you write "Yes" in a square, you can write "No" in every other square in that row and column.

2. Vanna has a pair of BananaBlade skates and a BananaBlower hair dryer. She can't decide which to give to Connie and which to give to Bonnie. Use this clue to help her decide:

☞ Bonnie won't dry her hair with anything but a towel.

	skates	hair dryer
Bonnie		
Connie		

Who gets the... **a.** BananaBlades? _____

b. BananaBlower? _____

3. Vanna, Old Man Nichols, and Ronny are going to a costume party. One will dress as an ape, one as a giant banana, and one as a bowl of Banana Flakes. But Cosmo's Costume Shop mixed up their costume orders! Use these clues to sort out the costumes:

☞ Old Man Nichols is always talking about monkeys.

☞ Vanna is allergic to breakfast cereals.

	ape	giant banana	Banana Flakes
Vanna			
Nichols			
Ronny			

Who dressed as the... **a.** ape? _____

b. giant banana? _____

c. bowl of Banana Flakes? _____

4. Vanna's kids, Dan, Jan, Fran, and Nan, all made banana inventions for their school's science fair. One made a banana phone. One made banana-flavored toothpaste. One made banana-peel bookmarks. One made a banana boomerang. But the name tags fell off the inventions! Use these clues, and draw your own logic box, to figure out who made what:

☞ Fran spends all her free time calling her friends.

☞ Dan and Nan don't take good care of their teeth.

☞ You can always find Nan at the library.

Who made the... **a.** banana phone? _____

b. banana-flavored toothpaste? _____

c. banana-peel bookmarks?_____

d. banana boomerang? _____

The Backward Burglar

Story Summary

Detective Tommy Tompkins must work backward after the Backward Burglar strikes a bank.

The Questions

Students must work backward to solve word problems.

Teaching Notes

Working backward help students to look at problems in different ways. It's easy to get locked into the idea that everything can be solved from left to right, top to bottom, beginning to end. At first glance, backward problems read like any other word problems. However, students will soon realize that they must start at the end of these problems and work toward the beginning.

SKILL/STRATEGY

Working backward

Additional Skills:
- Solving multistep problems
- Whole number +, −, ×, ÷
- Money +, −
- Working with time
- Measurement: pounds
- Reading for detail

◆ The Backward Burglar ◆

I got a call from the First National State Federal Trust Savings and Loan Bank of America. There had been a robbery. It wasn't just any robbery, though. The bank had been a victim of the Backward Burglar.

"Tommy, I'm glad you're here," said the bank manager when I arrived.

"Tell me exactly what happened," I said.

"It was very strange," said the manager. "A man came in the bank. He went up to teller number three, Doris. He gave Doris an envelope of money. Then he went to teller number two, Cloris. He gave her an envelope of money, too. Then he gave an envelope of money to Boris, who is teller number one."

"Sounds like the Backward Burglar to me," I said. "What happened next?"

"He went behind the counter, and emptied the three envelopes of money," the manager said. "He mixed it all up with our other money. Then he walked out of the bank."

It was a classic job by the Backward Burglar. He doesn't steal money from banks. He gives money to banks. That's because he's committing the robbery in reverse. No one understands him, but no one really minds.

"The burglar gave you extra money," I said. "So why do you need a detective?"

"We are a bank," the manager said. "We need to know exactly how much money we have. Now we have too much. And it's all mixed up, so we don't know how much extra money we have."

"The Backward Burglar usually leaves some backward clues," I said. "Did he say anything?"

"He told me he gave me $5 less than he gave teller number two," said teller number three, Doris.

"Well, he told me he gave me $10 more than he gave teller number one," said teller number two, Cloris.

"He told me he was giving me $6," said Boris, teller number one.

"Oh, it's all so confusing!" cried the bank manager. "How will we ever figure it out?"

I said it was simple to solve the problem. All we had to do was work backward. The last thing the burglar did was give Boris $6. Before that, he gave Cloris $10 more than he gave Boris. That means he gave Cloris $16, because $6 plus $10 equals $16.

The first thing he did was give Doris $5 less than Cloris. That means he gave Doris $11, because $16 minus $5 equals $11.

To find out the total amount of money the burglar gave to the bank, I just had to add up the three amounts he gave to Boris, Cloris, and Doris. So the Backward Burglar gave the bank $33, because $6 plus $16 plus $11 equals $33.

"You have $33 in extra money," I told the manager.

"You're welcome," said the manager.

"Ah-ha," I said. "A backward thank you."

The manager smiled. "You can bank on it."

NOW IT'S YOUR TURN...

Now work backward to solve the following problems. Do the math from the end to the beginning, just like Tommy did.

1. The Backward Burglar eats lunch in the middle of the day, just like everybody else. But he eats dinner in the morning and breakfast at night! Today, he ate 3 more Burglar Burgers than tuna fish sandwiches. He ate 4 less tuna fish sandwiches than bowls of cereal. The Burglar ate 6 bowls of cereal for dinner. How many Burglar Burgers did the Backward Burglar eat?

   _____

   _____

2. The Backward Burglar loves to sleep during the daytime. He snored for 4 hours longer than he talked in his sleep. He talked in his sleep for twice as long as he walked in his sleep. He walked in his sleep for 1 hour. For how many hours did the Backward Burglar snore?

   _____

   _____

3. The Backward Burglar has a backward backyard. That's because it's in his front yard! He has 3 times as many apple trees as shrubs. He has 5 more shrubs than swimming pools. He only has one swimming pool, right in the middle of his front yard. How many apple trees does the Backward Burglar have in his yard?

_____

_____

4. The Backward Burglar doesn't enjoy books very much. He always reads the endings first! He read 3 less pages in his cowboy book than he did in his science fiction book. The number of pages he read in his science fiction book was 1/2 the number of pages he read in his detective novel. He only read the last 20 pages of his detective novel. How many pages did the Backward Burglar read in his cowboy book?

_____

_____

5. The Backward Burglar was on a backward diet this week. He tried to gain weight! He gained 5 more pounds on Thursday than he did on Wednesday. He gained 5 times more pounds on Wednesday than he did on Tuesday. The pounds he gained on Tuesday were 1/4 the number of pounds he gained on Monday. On Monday, he gained 8 pounds. What is the total number of pounds the Backward Burglar gained on those 4 days?

_____

_____

The Cafeteria Caper

Story Summary

Detective Carmen Chang takes a sample of students in a school to estimate the number of suspects in a cafeteria case.

The Questions

Students use their class as a sample and predict the number of students in the entire school who have a variety of characteristics.

Teaching Notes

Taking a sample is an extremely useful statistical tool. The process can yield accurate predictions while saving a tremendous amount of time. Explain to students that whenever they see survey results, only a small portion of the population was actually questioned. The more people that are surveyed, the more accurate the results.

This lesson can also serve as a basic introduction to ratios and proportions. Let's say there are 5 redheads in a class of 30. The ratio of redheads to students in the class is 5:30, or $5/30$, or $1/6$. If there are 300 students in the school, a proportion can be written to estimate the number of redheads in the school:

$$\frac{1 \text{ redhead}}{6 \text{ students}} = \frac{x \text{ redheads}}{300 \text{ students}}$$

By cross multiplying, we can estimate that there are 50 redheads in the entire school.

◆ The Cafeteria Caper ◆

It was 12:30 in the afternoon, and I was starved. I accidentally left my lunch at home that day. I could picture that lunch bag, sitting on the kitchen counter. Just then, the phone rang.

"Come to the Candlewood Elementary School cafeteria," said a woman's voice over the phone. "We need a detective."

"This is Detective Carmen Chang. I'll be right over," I said, licking my lips. What a stroke of luck! I could solve a crime and have some lunch!

Harriet Hairnet met me at the cafeteria. She told me that she serves the food during lunch every day. She had been serving Tater-Tots that day. My mouth was watering just hearing about it! But Harriet said something went wrong. She had turned around to pick up a clean serving spoon. When she turned back around, the whole tray of Tater-Tots was gone. Someone had replaced it with a tray full of mothballs.

"Any suspects?" I asked.

"I'm not sure," answered Harriet. "I saw the kid for a second. It was a boy with red hair. But I didn't get a good look at his face."

 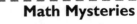

"Don't worry, Harriet," I said. "I'll find your thief if I have to talk to every redheaded boy in this school."

How much time would that take, I wondered? I was already starving! It would take me 10 minutes to speak to one kid, I guessed. What if there were 100 boys with red hair? I'd never get to eat lunch! I had to estimate how many redheaded boys there were in the school. The best way to do that? Take a sample! Here's what I did:

I went into Mrs. Brush's art class. There were 20 students in the room. I counted how many redheaded boys were in the room—just one. So I could estimate that 1 out of every 20 students in the whole school were redheaded boys. Mrs. Brush told me there were about 400 kids in the entire school. If 1 out of every 20 students was a redheaded boy, that meant there were about 20 redheaded boys in the school. There might be more, and there might be less. But by looking at a sample group of students, I could make a good estimate.

I figured I should get started interviewing the redheaded boys. I went to the desk of the one redheaded boy in Mrs. Brush's class, Moon Maroon. There was something on his desk covered with a sheet.

"Hi, Moon," I said. "I'm Detective Carmen Chang."

"I guess you found out that I stole those Tater-Tots," Moon said.

Wow! I found the thief on my first try! I was getting pretty good at this detective business. Better still, I could eat lunch soon!

"Moon, why did you steal all those Tater-Tots?" I asked.

"It's for my art project," he said. Moon lifted the sheet off the object on his desk. "It's a sculpture of Abraham Lincoln's head. Made completely out of Tater-Tots."

Moon paid for the stolen Tater-Tots out of his allowance money and apologized to Mrs. Hairnet. Harriet told me that she really didn't miss the Tater-Tots too much. She thought the mothballs tasted better!

NOW IT'S YOUR TURN...

Your class is a sample of your whole school! Find out how many students are in your entire school. For each item on the list, see how many kids in your class fit the description. Then predict how many kids in the whole school fit the same description. If you can, take a survey in your school to double-check your predictions.

Description	How Many in Your Class	Predicted Number in Your School
boys	_____	_____
girls	_____	_____
left-handed	_____	_____
right-handed	_____	_____
brown hair	_____	_____
black hair	_____	_____
blond hair	_____	_____
red hair	_____	_____
wear glasses	_____	_____
have a pet	_____	_____

YOU CAN DO IT What other categories would you like to find out about? Add them to the list and take a sample.

Keeping Track of Trains

Story Summary

Detective Chuck McBuck reads a train schedule to see if a man accused of stealing a train is telling the truth.

The Questions

Students read the train schedule to confirm or deny the accused train robber's story.

Teaching Notes

Reading a schedule is an extremely useful and necessary skill for everyday life. How often have you missed a train or bus because you didn't read the schedule correctly? Schedules can be very complicated, with different running times for rush hour, off-peak times, weekends, and holidays. The more practice that students can get at this skill at a young age, the better. Students may not even realize that there is math involved in this commonplace activity.

Leave Cleardale	Arrive Plattsburg
7:45 A.M.	8:25 A.M.
9:45 A.M.	10:25 A.M.
11:45 A.M.	12:25 P.M.
1:45 P.M.	2:25 P.M.
3:45 P.M.	4:25 P.M.
5:45 P.M.	6:25 P.M.
7:45 P.M.	8:25 P.M.
9:45 P.M.	10:25 P.M.

Leave Plattsburg	Arrive Cleardale
8:00 A.M.	8:40 A.M.
10:00 A.M.	10:40 A.M.
12:00 P.M.	12:40 P.M.
2:00 P.M.	2:40 P.M.
4:00 P.M.	4:40 P.M.
6:00 P.M.	6:40 P.M.
8:00 P.M.	8:40 P.M.
10:00 P.M.	10:40 P.M.

◆ Keeping Track of Trains ◆

Sure, I like being a detective, but I've always dreamed of being a cowboy. I could've been a great sheriff in the Old West. Riding my trusty horse, cooking over an open fire, and playing my harmonica. That's the life for Chuck McBuck! So I was excited when I heard there was a train robbery in our town. It was my chance to save the day, like a real cowboy! I rode my skateboard over to the Cleardale train station. A skateboard is not as good as a horse, but it gets the job done.

"You hardly hear of any train robberies these days," I said to the station manager, Rails O'Rourke. "It's hard to believe someone would get on a train and rob the passengers."

O'Rourke shook his head. "No one robbed any train passengers. I said there was a train robbery. Someone stole a train."

"A train?" I said. "That's a pretty big thing to get stolen."

"That's what I thought," said O'Rourke. "I left the station to buy some gum at 1 P.M. When I got back at 1:30, the train was gone."

I told O'Rourke that I'd check it out. My investigation led me to Al Abord, who works at Moe's Model Train Shop.

"Al, I think you stole a train yesterday," I told him.

"Why do you think that?" asked Al.

"There are two reasons," I told him. "One, you were spotted at the Cleardale train station before the robbery. And two, someone saw a train parked in your driveway yesterday."

"I was at the station yesterday," said Al. "I was taking a train to have lunch with my cousin in Plattsburg. Moe keeps track of my schedule. You can ask him when I left the store and when I got back."

"I'll ask him," I said. "And what about the train in your driveway, Al?"

"What? That thing?" said Al. "That must belong to one of the neighbors."

Moe showed me Al's schedule for yesterday. Sure enough, Al left the shop at 11:00 A.M., and came back at 2:30 P.M. I copied down the information and went back to the train station. I asked Rails O'Rourke for the daily train schedule between Cleardale and Plattsburg. Here's the schedule:

Leave Cleardale	Arrive Plattsburg	Leave Plattsburg	Arrive Cleardale
7:45 A.M.	8:25 A.M.	8:00 A.M.	8:40 A.M.
9:45 A.M.	10:25 A.M.	10:00 A.M.	10:40 A.M.
11:45 A.M.	12:25 P.M.	12:00 P.M.	12:40 P.M.
1:45 P.M.	2:25 P.M.	2:00 P.M.	2:40 P.M.
3:45 P.M.	4:25 P.M.	4:00 P.M.	4:40 P.M.
5:45 P.M.	6:25 P.M.	6:00 P.M.	6:40 P.M.
7:45 P.M.	8:25 P.M.	8:00 P.M.	8:40 P.M.
9:45 P.M.	10:25 P.M.	10:00 P.M.	10:40 P.M.

Rails O'Rourke told me that all the trains had run on time yesterday. I had to compare the train schedule to the times Al left and came back to Moe's Model Train Shop. When I accused Al of stealing the train, was I on the right "track"?

NOW IT'S YOUR TURN...

Help Chuck McBuck discover the train thief. Use the train schedule to answer the following questions.

Leave Cleardale	Arrive Plattsburg	Leave Plattsburg	Arrive Cleardale
7:45 A.M.	8:25 A.M.	8:00 A.M.	8:40 A.M.
9:45 A.M.	10:25 A.M.	10:00 A.M.	10:40 A.M.
11:45 A.M.	12:25 P.M.	12:00 P.M.	12:40 P.M.
1:45 P.M.	2:25 P.M.	2:00 P.M.	2:40 P.M.
3:45 P.M.	4:25 P.M.	4:00 P.M.	4:40 P.M.
5:45 P.M.	6:25 P.M.	6:00 P.M.	6:40 P.M.
7:45 P.M.	8:25 P.M.	8:00 P.M.	8:40 P.M.
9:45 P.M.	10:25 P.M.	10:00 P.M.	10:40 P.M.

1. If Al left Moe's Model Train Shop at 11:00 A.M., when does the first train leave that he could take from Cleardale to Plattsburg? _____

2. How long does a train trip take from Cleardale to Plattsburg?

_____

3. Say Al took the very next train back to Cleardale after arriving in Plattsburg. When would Al have arrived back in Cleardale? _____

4. Do you think Al was telling the truth about visiting his cousin? Why or why not? _____

_____

_____

_____

_____

_____

_____

_____

5. Say you wanted to spend the day with Al's cousin. You decide to take the train from Cleardale. What's the longest amount of time you could spend in Plattsburg and still return to Cleardale on the same day? _____

_____

YOU CAN DO IT Depending on how you answered question #4, write the ending of the story. What happened when Detective Chuck went back to talk to Al?

Chasing the Blues Away

Story Summary

Detective Cesar Hidalgo looks for patterns in street addresses to track down a person who's painting everything blue.

The Questions

Students find and complete a variety of number, letter, and picture patterns.

SKILL/STRATEGY

Finding patterns

Additional Skills:
- Whole number +, −, ×
- Visual discrimination
- Guess and check
- Using logic

Teaching Notes

Mathematicians have long been fascinated by patterns and sequences. Number patterns are found all around us in nature.

Some hints for finding patterns:

- Always read a pattern from left to right.

- Add, subtract, multiply, or divide the first number in a pattern to the number to its right. If the answer is the third number in the pattern, you may be on the right track. Test your guess to see if it works on the rest of the pattern.

- Some patterns may use more than one math operation.

- If the items in a pattern are shapes or symbols, pay attention to their size, shape, color, direction they're facing, how many there are, etc.

◆ Chasing the Blues Away ◆

It always happens this way: We won't get a single case for an entire week, and then suddenly we're the busiest place on Earth. The phone rings off the hook. All the detectives are running around like crazy. You know what they say—when it rains, it pours. And we don't have an umbrella! That's the kind of day it was when I took a call from Lester Chester.

"This is Cesar Hidalgo at the Effective Detective Agency," I said into the phone. "How can I help you?"

"This is Lester Chester," said the voice. "I'm real blue today."

"We all get sad sometimes, Mr. Chester," I said. "I'd like to cheer you up, but I'm real busy today. If you're blue, why don't you call Jiggles the Clown? He always cheers me up."

"I am sad," said Lester. "but that's not why I called. I'm really blue. I was taking a nap in the backyard, and somebody painted me blue."

It was another mysterious "blue paint" case! This was the fifth call we'd received that day! Mrs. Gamble called to say her dog was painted blue. Mr. Schnabel said his grandmother was painted blue. Charlie Drisko said his windows were painted blue. Lana Gershon said her lawn had been painted blue. And now Lester Chester, too!

"What's your address, Mr. Chester?" I asked.

"I live at 23 Sycamore Drive," said Lester.

"Try to wash off the paint, Mr. Chester," I said. "And we'll try to catch the mystery painter."

It was quite a mystery. Who was going around town painting everything blue? And why? And where would the painter strike next?

"Listen up everybody," I said to the other detectives. "I need to know where the other 'blue paint' victims live."

"Mrs. Gamble lives at 5 Sycamore Drive," said Tommy.

"Mr. Schnabel lives at 8 Sycamore Drive," said Gina.

"Charlie Drisko lives at 12 Sycamore Drive," said Chuck.

"Lana Gershon lives at 17 Sycamore Drive," said Carmen.

"And Lester Chester lives at 23 Sycamore Drive!" I said.

So all the victims live on Sycamore Drive. It was clear there was a pattern here. If I could figure it out, I would know where the painter would strike next!

I drew a diagram of Sycamore Drive on our chalkboard. I drew all the houses and marked the ones where the painter had struck. I wrote down the addresses of the victims' houses: 5, 8, 12, 17, and 23. The paint crimes happened in this order. The address number got bigger each time. But what was the pattern?

Then it hit me! Five plus 3 equals 8. There were 3 numbers between the first 2 "blue" houses. Eight plus 4 equals 12. So there were 4 numbers between the next 2 houses. Twelve plus 5 equals 17. Seventeen plus 6 equals 23. The amount of numbers between the victims' houses increased by 1 each time!

If this was the pattern, then there should be 7 numbers between the next two houses. Mr. Chester lives at 23 Sycamore Drive. Twenty-three plus 7 equals 30. So the next victim should live at...30 Sycamore Drive!

"Come on everybody!" I said. "We're going to 30 Sycamore Drive."

All the detectives raced down to Sycamore Drive. There were drops of blue paint all over the street. A blue dog barked. A blue Lester Chester snored in his backyard. Suddenly, we were in front of 30 Sycamore Drive. We were just in time! A little girl with blue hair was holding a paintbrush and a can of blue paint.

"Put down the brush!" I yelled.

"Rats!" said the girl. "I was about to paint the chimney blue!"

"Who are you?" I asked.

"I'm Little Girl Blue. Blue is my favorite color," said the girl. "I think everything should be blue."

"Blue is a nice color," I said. "But maybe not for dogs. And grandmothers. And lawns. And windows. Especially without permission."

Little Girl Blue agreed to clean up everything she painted blue. She also apologized to all the people and the dog. I'm sure glad I "brushed up" on number patterns!

NOW IT'S YOUR TURN...

Complete the patterns in the following problems.

1. The detectives didn't know it, but over on Mulberry Street, Red Reddington was on the loose! He painted these houses red: numbers 5, 10, 15, 20, and 25. What do you think are the next three houses Red will paint red?

    ——— , ——— , ———

2. Little Girl Blue painted this pattern on a wall.
Fill in the next three shapes.

■, ▲, ●, ◆, ■, ▲, ●, ◆, ____ , ____ , ____

3. Little Girl Blue painted over some of the letters in
the alphabet in her classroom! Here's what was left.
Fill in the next three letters.

A, D, G, J, M, P, ____ , ____ , ____

4. Little Girl Blue started painting squares of the sidewalk.
Complete the pattern.

□, ■■, □□□, ■■■■, □□□□□, _____ , _____ , _____

5. Cesar is the quarterback of his football team. He calls
out a number pattern before each play. Fill in the next
three numbers in Cesar's pattern.

40, 36, 33, 29, 26, 22, 19, ____ , ____ , ____

6. After being painted blue, Mrs. Gamble's dog started
barking in a weird pattern. Fill in the next three numbers
of barks in the pattern.

4, 12, 5, 8, 24, 10, 12, 36, 15, ____ , ____ , ____

YOU CAN DO IT Come up with your own pattern with numbers
or symbols. Trade with a classmate, and see if they can figure out
your pattern.

Crime on the Line

Story Summary

Detective Gina Jasper uses a logic line to find out the order of three robberies on Goose Street.

The Questions

Students make logic lines to put events in order.

SKILL/STRATEGY

Using a logic line

Additional Skills:
◆ Computing with time
◆ Reading for detail

Teaching Notes

A logic line is a great way to keep track of a sequence of events. Once again, we make a visual representation to sort out confusing details.

An easy connection can be made between logic lines and number lines. On a number line, lower numbers are to the left, and higher numbers are to the right. On a logic line, earlier events are to the left and later ones to the right.

Another great application of logic lines is to order historical events. This can lead to a cross-curricular research project.

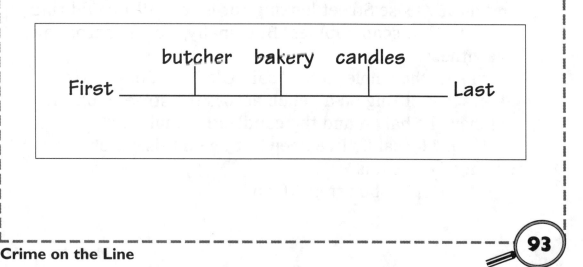

◆ Crime on the Line ◆

I'm Gina Jasper. Goose Street is usually a pretty peaceful place. That's why I was surprised to hear about three Goose Street robberies on the same day.

"They swiped three crates of lunch meat," said the butcher. "And that's a lot of baloney."

"They took all my dough," said the baker.

"They took the whole ball of wax," said the candlestick maker.

I had to find the people who robbed Butch's Butcher Shop, Anita's Bakery, and Candy's Candles. I went up and down Goose Street looking for clues. All I could find was a trail of soap bubbles. But finally, I came across an eyewitness.

"I saw the whole thing," said Old Man Peters. Mr. Peters was sitting on a bench across the street from the butcher, the baker, and the candlestick maker.

"Yep," he said. "I've been sitting on this bench, waiting for the bus."

"This isn't a bus stop," I said.

"That explains a lot," said Mr. Peters. "I've been sitting here for three days. That seemed like a long time to wait."

"So you saw who committed the robberies?" I asked.

"Strangest thing I ever saw," said Mr. Peters. "There were three men in a tub. A tub on wheels. They robbed those three stores."

Of course! It was Rob Adubdub and his brothers Bub and Grub! They always committed crimes in their "Bathmobile." That explained the trail of soap bubbles.

"I can catch the thieves," I said to Mr. Peters. "But you have to tell me exactly what happened."

"They robbed Candy's Candles after they robbed Butch's Butcher Shop," Mr. Peters said.

"So they robbed the butcher and went straight to Candy's Candles?" I asked.

"I can't remember," said Mr. Peters. "I do remember that they robbed Anita's Bakery before they went to Candy's Candles, but after they robbed the butcher."

Now Mr. Peters was starting to confuse me!

"Did I mention they were in a tub?" asked Mr. Peters.

"You did," I said. "Thank you, sir."

"Just checking," said Mr. Peters.

I really needed to know the correct order of the robberies! I could figure it out with the information Mr. Peters gave me. All I had to do was make a logic line.

I drew a line in my notebook with the word "first" on the left and "last" on the right. This would be my logic line.

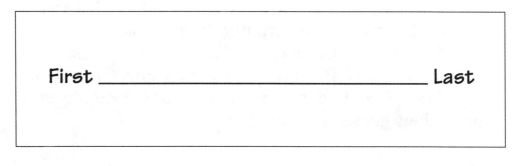

First _____ Last

Mr. Peters's first clue said that Candy's Candles was robbed after Butch's Butcher Shop. On my logic line, I wrote "candles" to the right of "butcher."

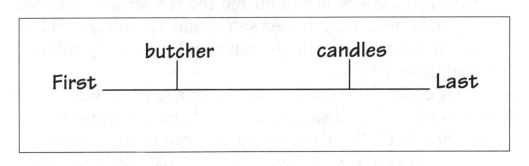

Mr. Peters's second clue said that Anita's Bakery was robbed before Candy's Candles. So "bakery" would be written to the left of "candles." But would I write "bakery" to the left or the right of "butcher"? Mr. Peters also said that the bakery was robbed after the butcher. So "bakery" would be written to the right of "butcher," but to the left of "candles."

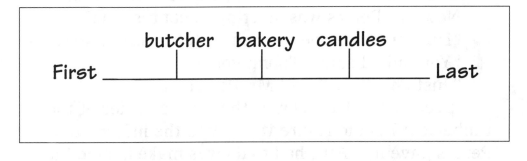

Now my logic line was complete. I knew that the butcher was robbed first, then the baker, and finally, the candlestick maker.

"That only leaves one question," said Mr. Peters.

Had I forgotten something? "What's that?" I asked.

"Where does the bus stop?" asked Mr. Peters.

I didn't know. But I did know one thing: Thanks to logic lines, I could catch the robbers of Goose Street. I guess their goose is cooked!

NOW IT'S YOUR TURN...

Use the clues in the problems to complete the logic lines.

1. One of the Adubdub brothers was born in 1969, one was born in 1970, and one was born in 1971. But who was born when?

   Clues:

   ☞ Grub was born before Bub.

   ☞ Rob was born after Grub.

   ☞ Bub was born after Rob.

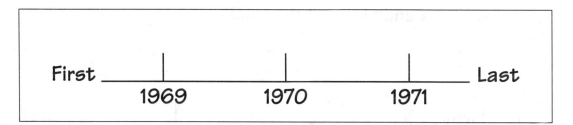

2. Gina looked for the Adubdub brothers in Soupy's Soap Shop, Huck's Rubber Duck Repair Shop, Howell's Towel Rack, and Wally's Water World. In what order did she go to the stores?

   Clues:

   ☞ Gina waded through Wally's before she visited Huck's or Soupy's.

   ☞ Gina peeked into Howell's after she made sure Soupy's Soap Shop was "clean."

   ☞ Gina ducked into Huck's before she entered Soupy's.

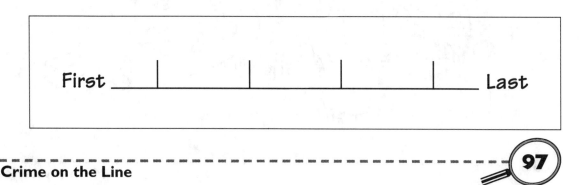

3. Between 2:00 P.M. and 3:30 P.M., the following events happened on Goose Street: Gina captured the Adubdub brothers, Soupy burst a bubble, Mr. Peters finally caught a bus, Candy burned a candle at both ends, and Anita crumbled a cookie. What times did the events take place?

Clues:

☞ Anita crumbled the cookie before Gina captured the brothers.

☞ Gina captured the brothers before Candy burned the candle.

☞ Soupy burst the bubble one hour and five minutes before Candy burned the candle.

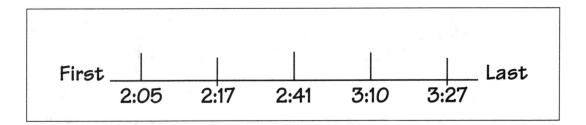

First _____|_____|_____|_____|_____|_____ Last
        2:05   2:17   2:41   3:10   3:27

YOU CAN DO IT Think of a few events from your life. Write a few clues to help someone figure out what order they happened in. Then have a classmate make a logic line to figure it out!

Who's Afraid of the Big Bad Mouse?

Story Summary

Detective Carmen Chang makes a table to see if a scientist's robotic mouse will catch up in size to a rapidly growing mouse.

The Questions

Students complete Carmen's table and answer questions based on the data.

Teaching Notes

"Making a table" is not a lesson in carpentry! This type of problem is also known in problem-solving lingo as an "exhaustive list." The concept is fairly simple: listing information until an answer is found. It is important for students to double-check their work. One missed calculation can throw off the rest of the list.

◆ Who's Afraid of the ◆ Big Bad Mouse?

Doctor Proctor is our town's local scientist and inventor. Some people think he's a genius. Most people think he's just nuts. Whenever one of his experiments gets out of control, he calls us at the Effective Detective Agency. Today he called me, Carmen Chang. I didn't mind. There's always something fun happening at Doc Proctor's place.

I arrived at Proctor's house and rang the doorbell. "Knock, knock, knock," went the bell. Proctor opened the door with a big smile on his face. "Do you like my new invention, the knocking doorbell?"

"It's, uh, very nice," I said.

"I knew you would like it!" said the doctor "Everyone likes the sound of knocking on a door. My invention gives you the sound but protects your knuckles." Doc Proctor's smile suddenly turned into a frown. "We can talk more about that later. I need your help with a little mouse problem. Or should I say, a big mouse problem."

I followed the doctor into his gigantic lab. A small puppy walked across the floor.

"What a cute puppy!" I said.

"That's not a puppy. It's a mouse," the doctor said.

"Ewww," I said.

"Let me explain," said Doctor Proctor. "Nicky, the mouse, was 2 inches long when I started this experiment. That was 10 minutes ago. I gave Nicky a growth formula. He's doubling in size every 5 minutes. He's 8 inches long right now."

"This could be a big problem," I said.

"You're right about that," added the doctor. "I built the walls of this house out of cheese. It was one of my first experiments. And it would make a nice little snack for a big bad mouse! Luckily, I may have the mouse situation under control."

"How's that?" I asked.

"I have a shrinking formula, Carmen," said the doctor. "I can't make Nicky drink it. But I built a robotic mouse that Nicky will follow. If the robot drinks the formula, so will Nicky."

Doctor Proctor showed me the robotic mouse, which was 1 inch long.

"Sounds like a great plan, Doc," I said.

"There's only one problem," said the doctor. "I made the robot too small." He explained that Nicky would only follow the robot mouse if the robot was bigger than Nicky.

"What are you going to do, Doc? That robot is way too small!" I said.

"I gave the robot a different growth formula,"

said the doctor. He said that the robot mouse, at the press of a button, could triple in size every five minutes. "I need you to help me figure out if the robot will catch up to Nicky's size. If Nicky grows for 60 minutes, he will burst out of this giant lab. He'll terrify everyone in town."

"Don't worry, Doc. I'll figure it out," I calmly said. "We just need to make a table."

"We don't have time to make a table!" screamed the doctor. "I don't even have wood or nails."

"Not that kind of a table," I said.

Here's the table I started:

MINUTES	NICKY'S LENGTH	ROBOT'S LENGTH
0	2 inches	not activated
5	4 inches	not activated
10	8 inches	not activated
15	16 inches	1 inch
20	32 inches	3 inches

NOW IT'S YOUR TURN...

Complete Carmen's table on page 102 to see if the mouse will destroy the house! See how long each mouse will get in 60 minutes. Remember, Nicky doubles in size every five minutes. The robot mouse triples in size every five minutes. When you're done, answer these questions.

1. Did the robot mouse get bigger than Nicky before the 60-minute deadline? _____

2. If so, how many minutes passed before it happened?

_____

3. How many inches bigger was Nicky than the robot after 35 minutes? _____

4. The Statue of Liberty is 151 feet tall. After how many minutes was Nicky longer than the Statue's height? (Hint: 12 inches equals a foot. Divide the number of inches by 12 to find out how many feet something is.)

_____

5. Suppose the robot got 4 times bigger every five minutes. Make another column on your chart to see the robot's new size. After how many minutes would the robot be bigger than Nicky?

_____

YOU CAN DO IT Based on the information in your table, write the ending to the story. Be sure to mention the sizes of Nicky and the robot. And don't forget the shrinking formula!

The Baseball Bandit

Story Summary

Detective Cesar Hidalgo has to "guess and check" with uniform numbers to prevent the Baseball Bandit from striking again.

The Questions

Students guess and check to solve a variety of baseball-related problems.

SKILL/STRATEGY

Guess and check

Additional Skills:
◆ Whole number +, −, ÷
◆ Reading for detail
◆ Critical thinking

Teaching Notes

We all use the "guess and check" method all the time, often without realizing it. It's simple trial-and-error: We try a certain solution, and if it doesn't work, we try another. On each successive attempt, we use the knowledge we've learned to make a better "guess." Guess and check can be used to solve almost every problem there is. And many times, it's the best way.

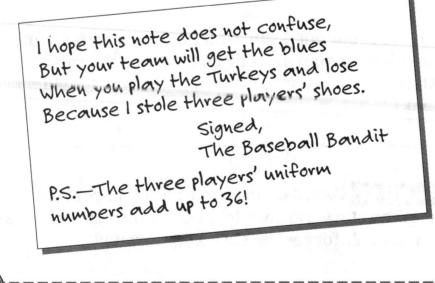

I hope this note does not confuse,
But your team will get the blues
When you play the Turkeys and lose
Because I stole three players' shoes.

Signed,
The Baseball Bandit

P.S.—The three players' uniform numbers add up to 36!

◆ The Baseball Bandit ◆

Everyone in town looks forward to baseball season. We all support our local team, The Dirt Stains. That's why I was really excited when I got a call from the Dirt Stains' manager, Leo McGraw.

"Somebody stole second base," said the manager.

"That's great, Mr. McGraw," I replied. "You've got some fast players on the team. It's going to be a great season."

"You don't understand, Cesar," said McGraw. "Someone actually picked up second base and left. It's gone! And I think there's going to be another robbery."

I rushed to the stadium to find out what was going on. Manager McGraw was waiting for me in the dugout.

"Don't worry about second base," said the manager. "We've got some extra bases. But we have to prevent the next robbery. The thief left a note. The shoes are the next target."

"Shoes?" I asked.

"Yeah, shoes. You wear them on your feet," said the manager. "Our first game is tonight. Without shoes, we won't be able to beat the Turkville Turkeys."

McGraw showed me the note. It said:

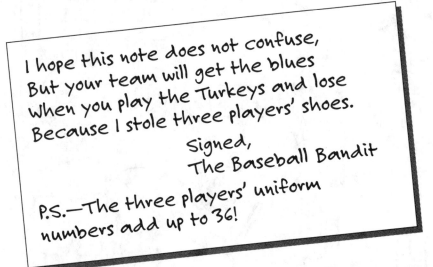

I hope this note does not confuse,
But your team will get the blues
When you play the Turkeys and lose
Because I stole three players' shoes.

Signed,
The Baseball Bandit

P.S.—The three players' uniform numbers add up to 36!

"If only we knew which three players the Bandit was talking about," said the manager. "Then we could protect those shoes."

"Maybe we can figure it out," I said. I asked McGraw for a list of his players and their uniform numbers. Here it is:

POSITION	NAME	UNIFORM NUMBER
pitcher	Lefty LaRue	21
catcher	Mac O'Reilly	7
first base	Scoop Davis	11
second base	Pepper Neal	33
shortstop	Tony Lonegan	14
third base	Mitch Martinez	42
left field	Ace Mahoney	3
center field	Reggie Weaver	27
right field	Stretch Humphrey	8

I knew I could find which three players' uniform numbers added up to 36. All I had to do was a little "guess and check." It's simple: Make a guess. Then check how close the guess is. Then make a better guess. Keep guessing and checking till you get it right!

For my first guess, I picked the first three players on the list: LaRue, O'Reilly, and Davis. Their numbers were 21, 7, and 11. That added up to 39. That was a little too high. Next, I added up LaRue, O'Reilly, and Mahoney: uniforms 21, 7, and 3. That added up to 31. That was too low. I thought for a little bit, and then tried LaRue, O'Reilly, and Humphrey: uniforms 21, 7, and 8. That added up to 36. Perfect! We put those players' shoes in a safe place till game time. The Baseball Bandit was foiled. But even with their shoes, the Dirt Stains lost to the Turkville Turkeys, 19 to 3. I visited the manager after the game.

"Tough loss, Mr. McGraw," I said.

"It was," said the manager. "But at least the Dirt Stains didn't get dirt stains on their socks."

As I left the stadium, I was sure the Dirt Stains were a "shoe-in" to be the champs this year.

NOW IT'S YOUR TURN...

Use the list of uniform numbers and the "guess and check" method that Cesar used to solve the following problems.

1. Now the Baseball Bandit wants to steal baseball mitts from three players whose uniform numbers add up to 78. Who are the players?

_____

_____

2. Next, the Bandit tries to steal the caps of four players whose uniform numbers add up to 66. Who are the players?

_____

_____

3. The player whose locker is to the left of Tony Lonegan has a smaller uniform number than Tony. The player to the right has a bigger number. Tony's number is right in the middle of the two other numbers. Whose locker is…

   a. to the left of Tony? _____

   b. to the right of Tony? _____

4. The team goes to a restaurant. Manager McGraw splits the players into two groups: One table of five, and one table of four. The total of the uniform numbers at both tables is the same. Who is sitting at…

   a. the table of five? _____

   b. the table of four? _____

5. Two new players join the team: Willie Amaze and Babe Ruthless. Their uniform numbers add up to 63. Babe's number is 5 more than Willie's. What is…

   a. Babe's uniform number? ___ _____

   b. Willie's uniform number? _____

THINK IT OVER Can you think of a way to solve problem #5 without "guessing and checking"?

Unlocking Lists

Story Summary

Detective Chuck McBuck makes a list to narrow down the combination of a safe containing the Dondello Diamond.

The Questions

Students make lists based on mathematical clues to find the combinations of various safes.

Teaching Notes

In these problems, students will be "making a list, and checking it twice." They will first list all possible solutions to the problem. With each clue, they will eliminate more answers, till they are left with only one. The problems also present an opportunity to cover various number concepts, including prime numbers, multiples, and factors.

SKILL/STRATEGY

Making a list

Additional Skills:
◆ Guess and check
◆ Whole number $+$, $-$, $\times$, $\div$
◆ Prime numbers
◆ Even/odd numbers
◆ Factors/Greatest Common Factor
◆ Multiples

◆ Unlocking Lists ◆

No one can ever accuse Chuck McBuck of having a piece of spinach stuck in his teeth. I take very good care of my teeth. As a detective, you never know when you might crack an important case. They'll want to put your face on the front page of the newspaper. And when you smile for the camera, you don't want everyone to see what you had for lunch. That's why I was flossing my teeth the other day when the phone rang.

"Mmmrrow," I said. "Miff isd Chudzt MiggBrttzz."

"What?" said the voice on the phone. "I can't understand a word you're saying."

I removed the dental floss from my mouth. "I'm sorry, I was just flossing my teeth. This is Detective Chuck McBuck. How can I help you?"

"This is Gladys Fluffington from the Fluffington Estate," said the voice on the phone. "You must come quickly. It's the Dondello Diamond."

"I'll be right there," I said. The Fluffingtons were the richest family in town. And the Dondello Diamond was the world's largest diamond. This was the case that could make me a star! Good thing I had flossed.

Mrs. Fluffington was waiting for me at the front gate. "It took you much longer than I expected."

"I ran out of mouthwash," I told her. "I had to buy some more before I came. So, you said that someone has stolen the Dondello Diamond?"

"Oh, no, you silly boy," Mrs. Fluffington laughed. "That would be awful. No, the diamond is very safe in its safe. The world's largest safe, of course."

I was confused. "So what's the problem, Mrs. F?"

"I've forgotten the combination," she said. "I want to show off the diamond at my tea party this afternoon. I need to get that safe open."

We walked through the Fluffington mansion to the safe in the laundry room. "Don't worry, Mrs. Fluffington," I said. "I forget my school locker combination all the time. Do you remember any part of the combination?"

"It's a complete blank," she answered. "But we did write down some mathematical clues about the combination, in case this ever happened." She pulled a piece of paper out her pocket. "It says that the combination has two numbers. The first number is a multiple of 3. It has 2 digits. They add up to 6. The second digit is twice the first digit. The second number in the combination is the first number divided by 8."

I studied the clues carefully. Then I pulled out my notebook. It would be easy to crack the combination if I made a list! The first number is a multiple of 3. In my notebook, I made a list of multiples of 3: They were 3, 6, 9, 12, 15, 18, 21, 24, 27, 30, 33, and so on. The combination number had 2 digits, so I could cross out 3, 6, and 9. And the number couldn't be greater than 99.

The next clue said the two digits added up to 6. Numbers 15, 24, 33, and 60 were also multiples of 3 that added up to 6. But the next clue told me that the second digit was twice the first digit. That means the number had to be 24!

Finally, I knew that the second number in the combination was the first number divided by 8. When 24 is divided by eight, the answer is 3.

"Mrs. Fluffington, I have the answer," I proudly said. "The combination of the safe is 24 and 3."

We opened the safe and took out the Dondello Diamond, just in time for the tea party.

"Are the newspaper reporters here?" I asked. "I'm ready to have my picture taken for the front page."

"There are no reporters here, you silly boy," said Mrs. Fluffington. "But you are welcome to stay for the tea party."

"No thanks," I said, as I got ready to leave. "Tea stains my teeth." Maybe my next case would get me on the front page!

NOW IT'S YOUR TURN...

Mrs. Fluffington has 2-digit combinations for the other 5 safes in the mansion. The Fluffingtons wrote down mathematical clues for each one. Can you make lists of numbers to figure them out?

1. Kitchen Safe

first number:
- ◆ An even number between 20 and 30.
- ◆ The two digits add up to 8.

second number:
- ◆ An odd number between 20 and 30.
- ◆ The two digits add up to 7.

The combination—first number: _____ second number: _____

2. Bedroom Safe

first number:
- ◆ A number between 1 and 10.
- ◆ The number is the same as the number of letters, in the number, when spelled out as a word.

second number: ◆ The first number times 9.

The combination—first number: _____ **second number:** _____

3. Basement Safe

    first number: ◆ A prime number less than 30.
                      ◆ The number minus 4 equals the
                         prime number before it.
                      ◆ The number plus 6 equals the
                         prime number after it.

    second number: ◆ Reverse the digits of the first number.

The combination—first number: _____ **second number:** _____

4. Living Room Safe

    first number: ◆ A factor of 36
                      ◆ Not a factor of 18
                      ◆ Not a factor of 24

    second number: ◆ The Greatest Common Factor of 20 and 24.

The combination—first number: _____ **second number:** _____

5. Attic Safe

    first number: ◆ A two-digit number
                      ◆ A multiple of 11
                      ◆ A factor of 308
                      ◆ The sum of the two digits added together
                       is a two-digit number.

    second number: ◆ Add together the two digits of the
                           first number.

The combination—first number: _____ **second number:** _____

A Picture-Perfect Mystery

Story Summary

Detective Tommy Tompkins draws a picture to figure out if Willy Whistle ate too much birthday cake.

The Questions

Students draw pictures and work with fractions to solve the word problems.

Teaching Notes

These problems give us yet another example of the benefits of visually representing a problem. To work through these problems without drawing a picture would involve some confusing fraction computation. But by simply drawing a picture showing each step, the problems become fairly simple.

In addition, these problems give students a good understanding of fractions, without getting bogged down in computation.

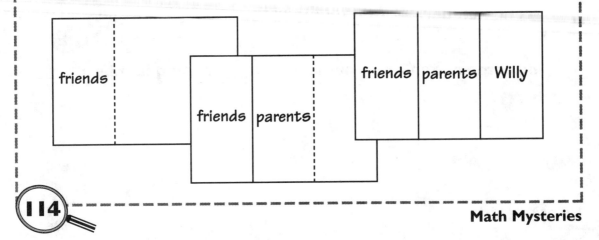

◆ A Picture-Perfect Mystery ◆

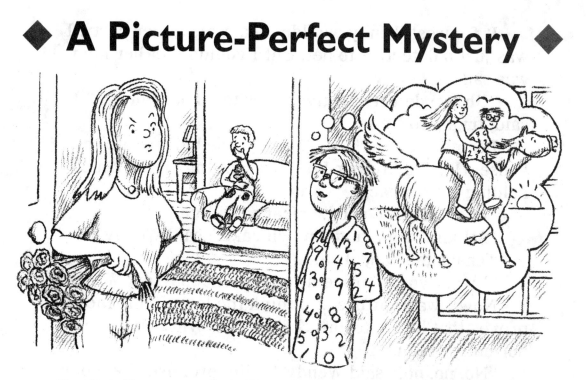

Don't tell anyone, but I've got a crush on Wendy Whistle.
She sits in front of me in Mrs. Beasley's class. And she's
the prettiest girl in the whole world. I haven't had the
courage to speak to Wendy yet. Every time I try, I just
freeze. So you can imagine how I felt when she called
me at the office.

"Hello, Tommy?" she said in her beautiful voice.
"Can you come to my birthday party? Right away?"

Wow! Wendy Whistle was inviting me, Tommy
Tompkins, to her birthday party! I didn't think she knew
I was alive! But she must like me, I thought. Why else
would she invite me?

"I'll be right over," I said. I put on my best shirt. I
got Cesar and Chuck to help me put on a tie. I went to
the flower shop on my way over and bought some roses.
I made sure my hair was okay and rang Wendy's
doorbell.

"Here you go," I said, handing her the roses as she
opened the door. "Happy birthday!"

Wendy looked confused. "Tommy, I need you to solve
a case. Why are you giving me roses?"

It figures! Wendy wouldn't want me at her party. I was just a detective to her. But I couldn't let her know I was sad.

"Uh, we detectives give roses to all our clients," I said, trying to smile.

I think she bought it. Anyway, she led me into the house. Her kid brother Willy was sitting on the couch, holding his stomach.

"I don't feel so good," moaned Willy.

"I think Willy ate too much cake," said Wendy.

"That's too bad," I said.

"I want you to prove he ate too much," said Wendy.

Now I was confused. "I think the look on his face proves that he ate too much," I said. "Willy isn't normally green."

"No, no, no!" said Wendy. "Willy promised he'd only eat 1/4 of the cake. But I think he ate more. You're a detective. I want you to prove it."

"I'll need some more information," I said.

"Here's all I know," said Wendy. "My friends ate 1/3 of the cake. My parents ate 1/2 of what was left. And Willy ate the rest."

I could solve this case by drawing a picture. I took out a piece of paper and drew a picture of the cake.

First, I marked the fraction of the cake eaten by Wendy's friends.

Next, I marked the fraction eaten by Wendy's parents.

My picture showed me how much of the cake Willy ate.

friends	parents	Willy

"I figured it out," I proudly said. "Willy ate 1/3 of the cake. That is more than 1/4 of the cake, which is what he promised to eat. So Willy ate too much cake!"

I was sure that I impressed Wendy with my detective skills. Now she knew what a great guy I was. I wondered how she would thank me.

"Thanks, Tommy," she said. "I'd give you some cake, but Willy ate it all. Can you leave now? I'm about to have another party."

I guess I didn't impress Wendy, after all. But thanks to drawing a picture, solving her mystery was a piece of cake!

NOW IT'S YOUR TURN...

Draw pictures, just like Tommy did, to solve the following problems.

1. Wendy tosses 1/4 of Tommy's roses in the backyard. She throws 1/3 of what's left in the trash. Willy eats the rest of the roses. What fraction of the roses did Willy eat?

2. Wendy keeps 1/5 of the gifts she receives on her birthday. She returns 1/2 of what's left to the store. Wendy gives the rest of the gifts back to her friends on their birthdays. What fraction of the gifts does Wendy give back to her friends?

3. Wendy invited 1/2 of Mrs. Beasley's class to her first party. She invited 1/2 of the remaining people to her second party. What fraction of the class didn't get invited to either party?

4. Willy finds a container of ice cream in the freezer. He eats 1/2 of it in the kitchen. He eats 1/4 of what was left up in his room. Willy puts the rest of the ice cream under his pillow for later. What fraction of the ice cream container is under Willy's pillow?

5. At Wendy's second party, the guests play games half of the time. They eat food for 1/3 of the remaining time. They watch Wendy open presents for 1/2 of the time that's left. What fraction of the time is left over to watch Willy turn green?

6. Back at home, Tommy gets out a school picture of Wendy. He uses 1/6 of his crayons to draw a mustache on her. He uses 3 times that number of crayons to draw worms in her hair. He uses 1/2 of his remaining crayons to give her monster teeth. What fraction of Tommy's crayons are left over?

YOU CAN DO IT Pick one of the problems and draw a picture to show what happened. Be sure to include the picture you used to solve the problem.

ANSWER KEY

A Soup-er Code (page 11)

1. BOWL
2. HALL
3. ONE
4. SPOON
5. 1 and 0
6. Q and Z

You Can Do It: Answers will vary.

A Small Misunderstanding (page 17)

1. c
2. c
3. a
4. b
5. c
6. Answer to 1: 73 pencils
   Answer to 2: $1.35
   Answer to 3: 14 inches
   Answer to 4: 9 pencils
   Answer to 5: 55 minutes

Think It Over: Answers will vary. To make sure you understand questions on school assignments, you could read them carefully, ask the teacher if you have any questions, and double-check your work when you're done.

Yard Work (page 23)

1. perimeter: 70 feet, area: 300 square feet
2. perimeter: 50 feet, area: 150 square feet
3. perimeter: 100 feet, area: 600 square feet
4. perimeter: 64 feet, area: 240 square feet
5. perimeter: 104 feet, area: 595 square feet
6. a. Wade Weeder's yard
   b. Rose Gardin's yard

You Can Do It: The perimeter of a standard 8.5 inch by 11 inch sheet of paper is 39 inches. The area is 93.5 square inches.

Think It Over: Answers will vary. Someone building a fence would need to know the perimeter of the yard. Someone buying seed or fertilizer might need to know the area of the yard.

Diving Into Mystery (page 28)

1. Mark Spritz, Wade Weeder, and C. P. Arr
2. Cloris Chlorine
3. Mark Spritz, Frank N. Mustard, Doreen Dryer, and Cloris Chlorine
4. Mark Spritz and Doreen Dryer
5. a. Wade Weeder, Doreen Dryer, or Cloris Chlorine
   b. Wade Weeder and Doreen Dryer
   c. Doreen Dryer

You Can Do It: Answers will vary.

Estimation Celebration (page 34)

1. a. 60 cans   b. 10 packages
2. 50 hamburgers
3. a–e. Answers will vary, depending on individual estimates.
4. Answers will vary. Cesar could guess about how much packages of each item will cost. Then he could add all the costs together. Cesar should probably bring more money than he estimates, in case his estimate is too low.
5. Answers will vary.

Think It Over: Answers will vary. You might need to know an exact number of something if you were selling items and wanted to keep track of how many you sold, or if you had a collection of items and wanted to make sure you hadn't lost any, or if you were counting money.

Too Much Talking! (page 39)

1. 6 minutes
2. 18 pages
3. 34 people
4. 42 bones
5. $.50

You Can Do It: Answers will vary.

Think It Over: Answers will vary. When you underline the important facts in a problem, you know what information to look at to solve the problem.

Watch Your Step! (page 45)

1. Two Steps: + and – Answer: 35 sets of footprints
2. Two Steps: × and + Answer: 30 pies
3. Two Steps: ÷ or × and + Answer: 37 minutes
4. Two Steps: – and –, or + and – Answer: $1.11
5. Two Steps: ÷ or × and – Answer: 6 slices

Good Buys for Spies (page 50)

1. $15.75
2. $12.50
3. 4 Finger Stingers
4. $211.35
5. $592.54
6. a–c. Answers will vary.

You Can Do It: Answers will vary.

Duck, Duck, Loose! (page 56)

Answers will vary. Make sure students' made-up facts tell…

1. …how many ducks Mal had all together.
2. …how far Snyder traveled.
3. …how many pounds the ostrich weighed.
4. …how many feathers Flip was missing.
5. …how long Cesar was at Mrs. Feathers' house.
6. …the height of the bump on Cesar's head.

You Can Do It: Answers will vary.

Tree Trouble (page 62)

1. 6 combinations
2. 6 combinations
3. 8 combinations
4. 4 combinations
5. 9 combinations
6. 30 combinations

You Can Do It: Answers will vary.

A Slippery Case (page 68)

1. Donny is the banana thief.

	red hat	yellow shirt	blue pants
Bonnie	Yes	No	Yes
Connie	Yes	Yes	No
Donny	Yes	Yes	Yes
Ronny	No	Yes	No

2. a. Bonnie   b. Connie

	skates	hair dryer
Bonnie	Yes	No
Connie	No	Yes

3. a. Old Man Nichols   b. Vanna   c. Ronny

	ape	giant banana	Banana Flakes
Vanna	No	Yes	No
Nichols	Yes	No	No
Ronny	No	No	Yes

4. a. Fran   b. Jan   c. Nan   d. Dan

	phone	toothpaste	bookmarks	boomerang
Dan	No	No	No	Yes
Jan	No	Yes	No	No
Fran	Yes	No	No	No
Nan	No	No	Yes	No

The Backward Burglar (page 74)

1. 5 Burglar Burgers
2. 6 hours
3. 18 apple trees
4. 7 pages
5. 35 pounds

The Cafeteria Caper (page 79)

Answers will vary.

Keeping Track of Trains (page 83)

1. 11:45 A.M.
2. 40 minutes
3. 2:40 P.M.
4. Al probably wasn't telling the truth. Moe's schedule said that Al came back to the shop at 2:30 P.M. If Al had visited his cousin, the earliest he could've returned to Cleardale would have been 2:40 P.M.
5 13 hours, 35 minutes

You Can Do It: Answers will vary.

Chasing the Blues Away (page 88)

1. House numbers 30, 35, and 40
2. ■, ▲, ◆
3. S, V, Y
4. ■■■■■■, □□□□□□, ■■■■■■■■
5. 15, 12, 8
6. 16, 48, 20

You Can Do It: Answers will vary.

Crime on the Line (page 93)

1.

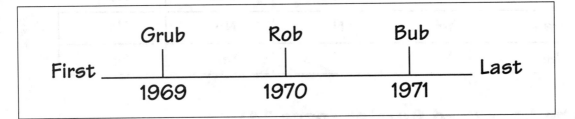

2.

First ____|____|____|____|____ Last

Wally's Water World | Huck's Repair Shop | Soupy's Soap Rack | Howell's Towel Rack

3.

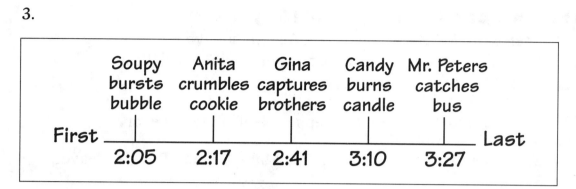

You Can Do It: Answers will vary.

Who's Afraid of the Big Bad Mouse? (page 99)

MINUTES	NICKY'S LENGTH	ROBOT'S LENGTH
0	2 inches	not activated
5	4 inches	not activated
10	8 inches	not activated
15	16 inches	1 inch
20	32 inches	3 inches
25	64 inches	9 inches
30	128 inches	27 inches
35	256 inches	81 inches
40	512 inches	243 inches
45	1,024 inches	729 inches
50	2,048 inches	2,187 inches
55	4,096 inches	6,561 inches
60	8,192 inches	19,683 inches

1. Yes
2. 50 minutes
3. 175 inches
4. 50 minutes
5. 40 minutes

You Can Do It: Answers will vary.

The Baseball Bandit (page 104)

1. Pepper Neal, Mitch Martinez, and Ace Mahoney
2. Lefty LaRue, Mac O'Reilly, Scoop Davis, and Reggie Weaver
3. a. Mac O'Reilly
   b. Lefty LaRue
4. a. Lefty LaRue, Mac O'Reilly, Pepper Neal, Tony Lonegan,
   and Stretch Humphrey
   b. Scoop Davis, Mitch Martinez, Ace Mahoney, and Reggie Weaver
5. a. 34
   b. 29

Think It Over: Answers will vary. You could write two equations: $x + y = 63$ and $x = y + 5$. Combining the two equations, we find that $2y + 5 = 63$. Solving the equation, we find that $y = 29$. Plugging that value into one of our original equations, we find that $x = 34$.

Unlocking Lists (page 109)

1. first number: 26
   second number: 25
2. first number: 4
   second number: 36
3. first number: 23
   second number: 32
4. first number: 36
   second number: 4
5. first number: 77
   second number: 14

A Picture-Perfect Mystery (page 114)

1. $1/2$ of the roses
2. $2/5$ of the gifts
3. $1/4$ of the class
4. $3/8$ of the container
5. $1/6$ of the time
6. $1/6$ of the crayons

You Can Do It: Answers will vary.